Advance p

"Jeff has a remarkable gift
in clear, understandable ways. This may be his ...
yet as he turns his attention to a topic that keeps so many people
from knowing God and his peace."
—Patrick Lencioni, author, *The Five Dysfunctions of a Team*

"Through engaging stories and winsome humor, Jeff Cavins communicates sound biblical advice for understanding suffering and its purposes. Drawing also on the wisdom of the saints—from Augustine to John Paul II—his book offers much-needed hope to readers and invites them to 'offer it up' in union with Christ."
—Rev. Pablo T. Gadenz, associate professor of
biblical studies, Seton Hall University

"Anyone committed to the New Evangelization will discover in *When You Suffer* a practical and profound resource that embodies Pope Francis's vision of the Church as a "field hospital" for the suffering and lost. Cavins's intelligence, honesty, and humor shine a hopeful light on a heavy and difficult obstacle to faith for many people."
—Rev. Michael White

"Suffering is not something we can avoid in this life. But it is something God can use for our good—if we let him. In this engaging book, Jeff Cavins beautifully shows us how to experience God's comfort, guidance, and strength in moments of suffering. Whether it be in the little inconveniences and frustrations we face every day or when our lives are completely turned upside down, Jesus wants to meet us in the crosses we face and help us find new light, especially when we fear all has become dark."
—Edward Sri, author, *Men, Women and the Mystery of Love*

"We have a pressing need in our Church today for a theology of suffering, and Jeff Cavins has responded to this need. In *When You Suffer*, Cavins presents a compelling synthesis from Scripture and Tradition that is not just necessary but incredibly useful. I can think immediately of ten people to whom I'd give a copy of this book."
—Fr. James Mallon, host of EWTN's *Cross Training*

"Cavins takes on a perennial enigma of the human experience with much scriptural insight and spiritual wisdom. The words of St. Gianna Molla capture the heart of the message, 'One cannot love without suffering or suffer without loving.' And his suggestions for 'offering it up' are particularly compelling."

—Bishop Michael Byrnes, auxiliary bishop
of the Archdiocese of Detroit

"*When You Suffer* helps the reader to approach suffering in a realistic and honest manner. In a confused and impatient world, this book is a welcome remedy. It's not just about suffering, it's about the way we live and understand living. Jeff Cavins has given us a tool that is relevant, smart, and personable."

—FR. RANDY DOLLINS, vicar general of
the Archdiocese of Denver

"Jeff Cavins has written an excellent book which sheds the profound light of the Scripture on that most universal of human realities, suffering. Read this yourself and give to your friends. This book will help tears turn into joy."

—RALPH MARTIN

"Jeff Cavins has written a solid, practical, book of biblical wisdom about handling the big and little suffering that come our way as Christians. Besides Scripture, he draws on the *Catechism* and the writings of the saints, especially St. John Paul II. It's easy to read, covers the territory, and is not too long. I plan on consulting it the next time suffering crosses my path!"

—DR. PETER S. WILLIAMSON, professor of sacred Scripture,
Sacred Heart Major Seminary

"Suffering can be destructive or redemptive. Jesus forever defeats destructive suffering through the mystery of his cross and resurrection. Jeff Cavins teaches this through specific helps based squarely on Scripture."

—JOHN MICHAEL TALBOT, founder of the
Brothers and Sisters of Charity

WHEN YOU SUFFER

[signature]

Gal 2:20

WHEN YOU SUFFER

Biblical Keys
for Hope and Understanding

JEFF CAVINS

servant

AN IMPRINT OF
FRANCISCAN MEDIA
Cincinnati, Ohio

LIBRARY OF CONGRESS CATALOGING-IN-PUBLICATION DATA
Cavins, Jeff.
When you suffer : biblical keys for hope and understanding / Jeff Cavins.
pages cm
Includes bibliographical references and index.
ISBN 978-1-61636-870-8 (alk. paper)
1. Suffering—Religious aspects—Christianity. 2. Catholic Church—Doctrines. I. Title.
BT732.7.C39 2015
248.8'6—dc23
2015024623

ISBN 978-1-61636-870-8

Published by Servant, an imprint of
Franciscan Media
28 W. Liberty St.
Cincinnati, OH 45202
www.FranciscanMedia.org

Printed in the United States of America.
Printed on acid-free paper.
16 17 18 19 5 4 3

Contents

FOREWORD

God is a Father who provides for his children. In his wisdom he allows us to suffer; but in his mercy he gives us great comforts—first and foremost in his Word, Sacred Scripture. Nothing enables us to make sense of human experience so well as the Bible does. In fact, I'd say that nothing but the Bible possesses that kind of explanatory power—especially when we are suffering.

The second great comfort God give us is our friends. God created us for the sake of love, and he made our human loves to be an image and a foretaste of his eternal love. God himself is relational and interpersonal. Thus Christians experience true friendship as an actual grace—an icon of the Trinity and a share of divine life.

It has been my privilege to count Jeff Cavins as a friend—as a comfort in suffering; as an actual grace. I do not need to count him separately from God's comfort, because Jeff is himself a profound interpreter of God's Word. When he speaks a word of consolation, when he offers a word of counsel, he draws from the only source we know to be divinely inspired and wholly inerrant. What is more powerful than God's Word delivered in friendship, delivered in love, delivered in charity?

It pleases me that you, too, will know the joy of Jeff's friend-ship through the pages of this book. Every page rings with authenticity because Jeff has suffered much and has learned through his suffering. To write such a book could not have been easy for him. It is an act of compassion in the root sense: a suffering-together with us.

C.S. Lewis said: "God whispers to us in our pleasures...but shouts in our pains."[1] We are often too wrapped up in ourselves to notice either. Our truest friends are those who help us to listen. Jeff is such a friend—to me and now to you, too.

—Scott Hahn

Chapter One

YOUR IDEAL LIFE

You picked up this book because you want to know if there is any meaning in suffering. Either you, a friend or a family member has suffered, and it has raised many questions in your mind. I want to tell you right away, yes, there is meaning in suffering if the suffering is joined with the suffering of Christ. In human suffering there is an immeasurable treasure, and that treasure has the power to assist in the redemption of mankind. I have to tell you right up front: If you knew how God could use your suffering—if you understood the heavenly "cash" you possess in your suffering—you would lose your fear and would actually embrace it, for even your very suffering has been redeemed.

Before we talk about the suffering that is at the level of crisis and agony, let's start with the low-grade frustration, the annoyances we experience on a day-to-day basis and then move up to the big-ticket items. Let's talk about your less-than-ideal day.

Take a moment to think about what you would consider your ideal life. You most likely started daydreaming about your ideal life when you were very young. As you grew up, the activities, relationships, and things that constituted your ideal life changed, but nevertheless you could probably articulate and describe your dream world to others.

What constitutes your ideal day? My guess is you could easily come up with a list of things that would make your day ideal. We all have our ideal day. For instance, I have an idea of what I'd like my day off to be like. I'd start by waking up refreshed in the morning after a good night's sleep. I'd take a walk to the local coffee shop with my Bible, where I'd sit down, have a cup of coffee, and read a portion of the Gospel. Maybe I'd visit with other early morning coffee drinkers, listen to a little music, and walk back home, where my kids would still be asleep. Next I would mow the lawn—or even better, take a ride on my Harley around the beautiful Minnesota lakes. Your ideal day might look totally different, but it will contain similar qualities. Let's look at what, for many, makes an ideal day—and an ideal life.

An ideal life is comfortable. We all want to have a comfortable life, a life that is satisfying, enjoyable, and peaceful. You want your day to feel like that favorite pair of jeans.

An ideal life is predictable. You know that when you get up, you're going to do certain things; you can count on this—you won't be caught off guard with any surprises. Your day will go just as you imagined it would the day before.

An ideal life involves being engaged in your personal interests. You might like to read and take walks; you might be interested in motorcycling or woodworking or gardening. It's what you would want to do given the spare time.

An ideal life reflects your gifts. Maybe you're a gifted musician or artist, or you might be a gifted writer or speaker or businessperson. Walking in your giftedness gives you the opportunity to shine.

An ideal life is affirming. In your ideal life composed of ideal days, people affirm you. You are seen as valuable and others recognize your contribution. Hearing that others affirm your value leaves you with a sense of fulfillment.

An ideal life is pain-free. No one likes pain. You want your days full of pleasure and good health. A blistering sunburn, an aching back, or an excruciating headache certainly are not found in your ideal day.

An ideal life brings a sense of accomplishment. You feel like you are making progress in your life; you complete projects and attain your goals. Your only problem here is where to put the awards and plaques that reflect your achievement.

An ideal life meets your basic needs. The basic needs for rest, nourishment, and stimulation are met. There's money in the bank and food in the refrigerator. Your relationships are fulfilling and life is good.

But there's a problem with ideal life—it's called real life. The problem with your ideal life is that you have to wake up and face reality. One by one, real life whittles away at your list of ideals, leaving you with a less than ideal life. Let's look at the differences.

Real life is uncomfortable. You might not be comfortable with what is facing you today for a variety of reasons. Your meetings or tasks tomorrow just may cost you your good night's sleep.

Real life is unpredictable. It might not be what you were expecting. There are conflicts with your schedule, unexpected emails that show up in your inbox, and instant messages and phone calls and kids... Today became an unpredictable day. Real life was interrupted by an uninvited intruder. .

Real life is uninteresting. Suddenly you realize you have to go to your daughter's dance competition, which will last five hours even though her dance is only three minutes. This all when you were planning on going fishing with your friends. Doing your taxes, the boring parts of your job—real life has many aspects that don't interest you.

Real life doesn't maximize your gifts. Too often you are stretched thin or pulled out of your comfort zone to attempt something you're not confident doing. You might be ready to cook a great meal, something you're gifted at, but one of your children needs help getting the chain back on his bike, something you fumble with.

Real life is unaffirming. There's no guarantee that you will be recognized for your contributions or affirmed for your value. Often the good you bring may very well go unnoticed.

Real life is painful. You slip on the ice while getting into your car and break your wrist. Suddenly pain is a part of your day. In fact, it will be for the next two months, at least until the cast is taken off.

Real life lacks a sense of accomplishment. You serve your family and work at your job, and yet at the end of a day you don't feel you've accomplished much of anything. Your email inbox mocks you, and your uncut lawn waves at you every time you look out the window.

Real life includes unmet needs. In some cases your needs do not get met. You rushed to get ready for work and had to skip breakfast. You don't have enough money at the end of the month to pay all your bills.

Less-than-ideal lives and situations are the lifeblood of newspapers, radio, and TV newscasts. They feed on it. The headlines do not usually highlight what people have accomplished but rather what they have suffered, as if suffering is the real news that breaks into our ideal world. A man was robbed, a woman was assaulted, a bomb exploded at the finish line of a race, or a city is leveled by a tornado. In addition, the stories we hear about and share at the water cooler are tragedies that were completely unexpected. It's not supposed to happen; it's shocking and takes the victims unaware. Suffering makes for great newscasts because it's unexpected, out of the ordinary, and oftentimes undeserving. In short, your bad news is good news for the evening news.

When real life collides with your ideal life, things can get ugly. You might react in a less than Christlike way. You might think your ideal life is what you deserve as an American; there is a deeply embedded sense of entitlement to "the good life." In response to real life you can tranquilize yourself, immerse yourself in a hobby, or get lost in books. At times you might even make those around you pay the price for your misfortune. The following is an example from my own life.

My Ideal Day
I had an ideal Saturday ahead of me. I looked at the calendar; there was nothing going on. The blank Saturday on my Google calendar looked like a refreshing and much-needed oasis in the desert. While my wife and daughters were still asleep, my plan was to take my motorcycle out for an early morning ride. After my joy-filled ride, I thought I would clean the garage—which might not sound like an enjoyable way to spend a Saturday, but

for me, tasks like this are fun. Because I'm usually involved in writing and speaking and meetings, it's actually a bit of a luxury to have the time to get things done around the house and yard. For lunch maybe I'd get some brats and throw them on the grill. Later I thought I could treat the family to a movie and then pizza. In my mind, this was going to be a great day.

But as I was about to leave on my bike, I realized that my wife was up. It looked like she was getting ready to go somewhere. I ask her what she was doing up so early, and she answered, "Don't you remember?" My mind instantly went blank, quickly searching for what she was about to surprise me with that would no doubt ruin my day. "We're going to my cousin's best friend's daughter's wedding today." Stunned, numb, and with my emotions starting to feel like a volcano rumbling, I said in a condescending voice, "No, I did not remember." I pointed out to my wife that there was no mention of this event on the calendar. Suddenly reality hit me.

Others often pay the price when real life collides with ideal life. And this particular Saturday, that's what happened in my home. I blamed my wife for ruining my plans, and I made her pay on the hour-and-a-half drive to the wedding. I wanted to make sure she knew that she'd better not do something like this again; I wanted to make it crystal clear that next time events like this would appear on the calendar. In case there was any doubt in her mind, I let her know that I do not deal well with uncomfortable, unpredictable, uninteresting, painful, unaffirming situations in my life. And what about the example I set for my children? Basically I communicated to them that the way adults deal with real life is pretty similar to the way kids tend to react when they don't get what they want or they're asked to clean their room or do their homework. Well, I made sure my wife knew exactly what I thought—but as a result, any peace and joy I had been feeling earlier that day quickly disappeared.

Virtual Life

When real life hits ideal life, many individuals are tempted to retreat from reality. Did you know that there is an entire online community known as Second Life? Members create ideal avatars of themselves, and they create an entire fantasy life for themselves—how they look, what kind of personality they have, what type of friends they enjoy, where they work, where they live, etc. This virtual life becomes more meaningful—and perhaps more real than real life. Just a few years ago, a man in "First Life" (better known as real life) took another man to court over some real estate transactions in Second Life.[1]

Robert Geraci, the author of *Virtually Sacred: Myth and Meaning in World of Warcraft and Second Life*, writes that, based on his research, many religious communities have popped up in Second Life, with players building churches, temples, and meditation gardens. One of the groups Geraci discovered in Second Life was a community focused on C.S. Lewis's *Chronicles of Narnia*, with its members exploring the Christian themes of the novel and connecting them with modern religious ideas. Finding a group like this in real life would be tricky, Geraci argues.

> "Second Life enables someone to have a Christian community, like the Christian Narnian landscape, that would be fundamentally impractical and probably impossible in the conventional world," he says. "From

a religious perspective, people are making their lives rich and meaningful and interesting in these virtual worlds."[2]

It's clear that people are seeking ideal lives: rich, meaningful, and shared with others. Yet the only way many can find to achieve this is through a virtual world that is far removed from their day-to-day, real-life existence. This is a great illustration of how badly we want to escape from reality. Escaping to fantasy can also go terribly bad when people escape to a virtual life of sin, such as pornography, gambling, or illicit relationships. Along with this type of fantasy, people also escape by self-medicating and going on dangerous adventures.

Perhaps the most disastrous result of not dealing with real life in an appropriate way is this: We respond by living a partial life. If we are honest, we might admit that we are really only living a third of our life—we merely put up with the other 60 percent—we just go through the motions. We embrace the good times and are truly thankful for them. But as for the rest of our schedule? We just put up with life, waiting in quiet frustration for the next ideal moment. We put up with our spouses, our kids, our jobs, our health issues, our financial struggles. This is living a partial life.

One Hundred Percent Life
But what if instead you discovered that you could live 100 percent of your life? Would you be interested in learning a new way of dealing with real life when it hits your ideal life? Would you like to know how to turn real life into ideal life? What if real life could be transformed into an opportunity to love, an opportunity to grow, and an opportunity to become more like

Christ? What if you could turn your real life into an opportunity to experience joy, peace, and contentment? What if your real life became a stage on which your children or grandchildren learned valuable life lessons?

The first step, though, is recognizing the fact that real life involves suffering. You might say, "Wait a minute—I don't have cancer; I've got a job, a nice house, I'm still married…one of the kids has some problems, but we're doing OK."

But if you took a step back and were really honest, you might admit that a certain percentage of your life could be classified as a kind of low-level suffering. You aren't really happy with aspects of your situation, whether at work or at home. In the following pages, I'll show how all of us have an opportunity for our daily (i.e., real) lives to be transformed, whether it is through intense suffering or a dull, nagging type of suffering. When life gets uncomfortable, unpredictable, when you feel weak and empty—that's exactly when you have an opportunity to become more like Christ. The mystery of suffering is that out of this weakness and emptiness, out of this less than ideal life, can come incredible graces. Christ is the key to transforming suffering into much more of an ideal life than you could ever imagine. Transforming a less than ideal life into real life is one of the great secrets that Christ wants to give you. When you discover this secret and walk in it, those around you will want to know how you do it. In short, tough times can be an opportunity to not only grow in Christ but an opportunity to help others who struggle with their ideal life.

Real life—not some virtual life counterfeit—is your opportunity to love and model Christ to the world. We sometimes forget that as Christians, we are called to live a Galatians 2:20 life: "I have been crucified with Christ; it is no longer I who live, but Christ who lives in me; and the life which I now live in the flesh I live by faith in the Son of God, who loved me and delivered Himself up for me." Christ's cross is the perfect expression of love. All those things that don't measure up to your ideal life can be transformed into Christ's likeness. So often, though, we ignore or reject the opportunity to turn to Christ and be transformed. We miss the opportunity to die to ourselves and let Christ shine in and through our daily lives.

Since Jesus's death on the cross is the full expression of love, we have to ask ourselves how real love feels. We are living in a culture that typically ties happiness to feelings. (We'll talk more about this later.) But all the obstacles and trials of life, which we perceive as making us unhappy, are not impediments to real living; instead they are ways of really living, opportunities to discover that real living involves real loving and real loving can be painful at times. When we see this, we stop treating our trials as things we have to deal with before we can do what we really want to do. We stop seeing our less than ideal days as necessary pauses on the way to ideal life. We stop seeing other people's inadequacies as roadblocks to prevent us from living the life we really desire to live.

There's really only one way to understand our suffering, and that is to understand Christ's suffering. Jesus said in John 15:13, "Greater love has no man than this, that a man lay down his life for his friends." Now, this sounds uncomfortable, most likely unpredictable, not very affirming—and most of us are not interested in dying anyway.

Many people today, whether they acknowledge it or not, have their own religion, and they like to think it works for them. Many TV talk shows and popular books espouse a personalized philosophy of life that they claim works for them. Often we hear friends, family or acquaintances proudly talk about their keys to living. But when they encounter unwanted circumstances, a deeper look reveals that their keys really don't unlock anything for them. Yes, they may have some valuable insights about success or how to become the best you possible, but when it comes to suffering, life remains a mystery. They don't know how to deal with suffering. At best, many just end up tolerating their less-than-ideal life, which is a subpar way to live. Archbishop Charles Chaput wrote, "Jesus said the truth would make us free. He did not say it would make us content or wipe away life's ambiguities."[3]

No Way to Escape Suffering

From the beginning humans have been plagued by the question of suffering. Why would God let bad things happen to good people? We ask ourselves, "If God is a loving, caring God, why does he allow suffering? When you or I suffer, we wonder, "Did I bring this suffering on myself, and is there any value in it at all?"

As we look through salvation history in the Bible, we can discover several purposes for suffering, but it is not until we come to Christ that we understand the full redemptive dimension of suffering. Christ Jesus conquered suffering by love. Because we are joined to him, our own suffering takes on redemptive value. Paul understood this, and so did Mary, the mother of Our Lord. When we understand this, we then have the choice to love as Christ loves. Through the sacrifice of the Mass, we have the opportunity to join our sufferings to Christ's sufferings, to fill up that which is lacking in his afflictions for the sake of the Church. We can embrace our sufferings and love like God loves. There, on the altar of the New Covenant, our sufferings truly make sense—and only there.

Through a mystery that can only be known through experience, our trials are turned into joy—and that joy is our strength. We learn that in the times of trial God's grace—that is, the very life of the Trinity—is sufficient for every situation. Through suffering, we reach out to God in prayer. He increases and we decrease. The apostle Paul said:

> I have learned, in whatever state I am, to be content. I know how to be abased, and I know how to abound; in any and all circumstances I have learned the secret of facing plenty and hunger, abundance and want. I can do all things in him who strengthens me. (Philippians 4:11–13)

Suffering is universal. We all experience it—if not today, then at some point in the future. Divorce, cancer, car accidents, the loss of a child, a parent, a job—these are all part of being human. Kids suffer, too. They are humiliated or bullied at school; many don't have a stable home life. Any of us might be the target of gossip or experience heart problems or live through a hurricane. The question is not *if* you are going to suffer, but *when*.

But more importantly, *how* will you suffer?

Some of the closest disciples of Jesus missed the meaning of the passion because it was not what they expected. They were expecting Jesus to be a triumphant king, not crucified like a common thief. We have our own set of expectations regarding life. We plan to live in a house in the suburbs with a picket fence, two cars, and three kids. We are not expecting to lose a job, deal with cancer, or break our leg in a bicycle accident. If you are married, on your wedding day, my guess is that you did not see any of this as part of your future either.

The Meaning of Happiness

Before we look at the problem of suffering and discover the keys to understand it, we have to address the modern notion of happiness. Our definition of happiness today is much different than how the ancient philosophers, such as Aristotle and Plato, viewed it. In Peter Kreeft's excellent book, *Making Sense Out of Suffering*, he tells us that the ancient philosophers saw it as an objective state, not a subjective feeling. As Kreeft writes, "Happiness is not a warm puppy. Happiness is goodness."[4] In other words, to be happy is to be good. The Greek word for happiness is *eudaimonia*, which literally means "good spirit," or "good soul."[5]

This is very different from the contemporary understanding of happiness. In today's world, what gives one's life meaning is *feeling* good—feeling good, not *living* well. Feeling good is not compatible with suffering, while living a good life *is* compatible with suffering. Many of us actually set ourselves up for not being happy as we buy into the modern notion of equating happiness with feeling good. If my happiness is based on feelings, then I have to spend my day making sure that everything around me is designed to make me feel good. If I do not feel good, I am not happy. Suddenly, holidays become great sources for being unhappy as family conflicts arise. Unexpectedly the call from the school principal rains on your sunny parade. With the modern notion of happiness, sickness leaves no room for happiness in the human heart.

If you think of happiness as a feeling, when you experience suffering, you are unhappy. But if you think of happiness as living well, can you see how even during an experience of suffering, you might still be happy?

Today, however, the popular definition of being good is being kind. In other words, a good person does not do anything that would make others suffer. By this standard God is not good if he lets us suffer. Because today we find it difficult to make the distinction between subjective and objective happiness, we find it hard to believe in a God who lets us suffer. Kreeft makes the point that "by ancient standards, God might be good even though he lets us suffer, if he does it for the sake of the greater end of happiness, perfection of life and character and soul, that is, self."[6]

Kreeft goes on to say, "A quick reflection on human parenting tells us that we know deep down that the ancient mind is right. Parents who want only freedom from suffering for their children are not wise parents."[7] Most modern parents know that allowing their children to suffer to some degree will result in a greater good when it comes to character. Paul's sums up his view of life in Romans 8:28 when he says, "We know that all things work together for good to those who love God, to those who are called according to his purpose."

Parents who put their children in a cocoon deprive them of the benefit of growing through trials. It is in trials that we strive for a better answer to our problem, we learn through a broken heart in teen years, and we face the consequences of poor study habits in our high school exams. The parent who acts as a buffer to life's difficulties only delays the inevitable struggle that will take place later, when the child is grown and out of the house.

Paul brings up a very important point in Romans 8:28. He writes, "We know that all things work together..." All things means all things. Once the mystery of suffering is understood, suddenly all things in life can be used for the greater good resulting in happiness. Without the knowledge of this secret, some things will remain outside the possibility of contributing to happiness. Putting it another way, when you understand the mystery of suffering, no longer do two thirds of your life have to be spent simply putting up with life. That two-thirds of less-than-ideal living can "work together for the good."

Two Kinds of Suffering

In his apostolic letter *Salvifici Doloris*, St. John Paul II says that "suffering is almost *inseparable from man's earthly existence*."[8] He defines two kinds of suffering: physical suffering and moral suffering. The distinction is based on the double dimension of the human being, the bodily and spiritual elements of humanity.

• *Physical Suffering*

Physical suffering is the kind of suffering we are all familiar with; it's when the body is in pain. It could be a cold, it could be cancer, it could be a broken limb, or it could be injuries from a car accident. Some kinds of physical suffering are specific to age and gender. Physical suffering is more out in the open, more difficult to mask or hide than other kinds of suffering.

Physical suffering can be a career-ending injury or a dull ache that depletes us of joy and vitality. My interest in the topic of suffering started in earnest when my C6–7 disk in my neck ruptured, landing me in physical agony. In my case, as many others could attest to, my physical suffering was coupled with moral suffering.

• *Moral Suffering*

Moral suffering is when the soul hurts. It might be the result of a betrayal. Maybe it's the loss of a loved one, or the loss of a job. Whatever triggers it, moral suffering means that our soul is hurting. Moral suffering is oftentimes hidden and not as noticeable as physical suffering, and many times it's harder to treat. The great classic by St. John of the Cross, *Dark Night of the Soul*, describes in detail the heart that is suffering in a spiritual or moral sense. Both Blessed Teresa of Calcutta and St. Padre Pio talk at length about their seasons of desolation and emptiness. St. Faustina describes in her diary how "the soul is engulfed in a horrible night."[9] All three of these saints experienced this kind of suffering, but the world was not aware of the depth of their suffering until after their deaths. Why? Because they knew what to do with it. We will learn more about this later in this book.

The Old Testament is filled with examples of both kinds of suffering, but particularly moral suffering. The danger of death. The threat of a flood. The death of a child. Infertility. Being exiled and longing for Canaan. Mockery and scorn. Loneliness and abandonment. Difficulty understanding why the wicked prosper. The unfaithfulness of a friend or neighbor. While we generally try to avoid any kind of suffering, given the choice, many people would choose physical suffering over moral suffering. Many would choose a broken leg over a broken heart.

Both kinds of suffering can leave us exhausted and bring us to the realization that we ultimately have our limits and cannot solve every problem in life. Suffering tells us, loud and clear, "You are not in control of your life; you are a victim." In one way this is true, for St. John Paul II tells us that suffering has a "passive character."[10] Suffering is something that happens to us, not something we do. While we do have control over many areas of our life, we often make careless or profoundly imprudent decisions that result in physical or moral suffering. But all too often, suffering happens to us as the result of circumstances that we couldn't control or foresee happening. Because suffering is "passive" in character, we often experience a sense of injustice or a "why me?" attitude. After all, if we had a choice, we would never have chosen this discomfort. It's like we want to yell as we exit the doctor's office, "All right...who is to blame here?" What we find in the end is that sometimes suffering is brought on by our decisions or lack of skill in a given area, but other times, suffering has no explanation as to its origin. We know one thing, though, and that is suffering happens, and it happens to us. What we will learn in the following pages is how to respond.

St. John Paul II describes the world of suffering as being divided up into many parts that exist "in dispersion."[11] He goes on to say, "Every individual, through personal suffering, constitutes not only a small part of that 'world,' but at the same time that 'world' is present in him as a finite and unrepeatable entity."[12] This means that *your* suffering is unique and unrepeatable. This will be important to remember later in the book when you will discover the keys of what to do with these unique and unrepeatable suffering events in your life.

While your suffering is unique, St. John Paul II reminds us that our suffering "possesses as it were its *own solidarity.* People who suffer become similar to one another through the analogy of their situation, the trial of their destiny, or through their need for understanding and care, and perhaps above all through the persistent question of the meaning of suffering."[13] In my early forties I had my neck fused as a result of a long and painful injury, which I mentioned briefly above. After my neck healed, it wasn't unusual for me to meet others who had had the same experience. It was uncanny—we understood each other without even saying a word. It was as if we were members of some secret club that only those who had suffered similar pain would understand. Our group saying was, "Been there, done that."

Two More Types of Suffering

In addition to physical and moral suffering, St. John Paul II differentiates between two other types of suffering. The first is *temporal suffering.* Temporal suffering is due to the consequences of sin—for instance, illness or physical death. It's suffering, but it's temporary. The second type of suffering is what the Holy Father calls *definitive suffering*:

> Man perishes when he loses eternal life. The opposite of salvation is not, therefore, only temporal suffering, any kind of suffering, but the definitive suffering, the loss of eternal life, being rejected by God, damnation. The only-begotten Son was given to humanity primarily

to protect man against this definitive evil and against definitive suffering.[14]

We know that God loved us so much that he sent his only Son to experience physical and moral suffering for our eternal well-being so that we would not suffer definitively or suffer forever without him. This is an expression of love, and we are meant to see that this is in some cases how love feels. Love is not just feeling good about a relationship or some kind of inner warm feeling—it's not all romance and everything always working out to our liking. Love can actually be quite difficult, painful, and sometimes devastating.

Jesus's Ideal Day

When we look at our ideal life meeting our real life, it does us well to think and contemplate on the life of Christ. What fulfilled Jesus were not earthly comforts, rather, it was to do his Father's will (see John 17). His ideal day was not so much about his schedule, his physical comforts, his leisure time, or his future. Jesus's ideal day was completely wrapped up in knowing and doing the will of his Father. Even on Good Friday, the day that Christ was crucified, ideal life was not associated with physical comfort or pain free living; it was associated with love and doing the will of his Father. The cross might not have been Jesus's ideal day as we typically measure ideal days, but it was his real life and it was real love, and it was really fruitful. In terms of the eternal outcome, his worst day ended up becoming our most ideal day as it relates to eternal happiness.

As you continue to read, I want to take this moment to encourage you. You aren't alone in your suffering or in your quest for understanding. The treasure you are searching for—the valuable meaning in your less-than-ideal day is a reality that can be experienced. You will find meaning attached to your suffering, meaning that will give you courage and purpose beyond anything you have known before. In addition, I will give you some powerful suggestions on what you can do in the midst of your suffering. Suffering is a terrible thing to waste!

Chapter Two

Is There Meaning in My Suffering?

$\mathbf{W}$hen life seems to be going according to plan, a myriad of unforeseen variables remind us that no life really does go according to a preconceived plan.

When bad things happen to good people, when tragedy strikes, when life throws us a curve, inevitably someone will ask the question, "Why? Why do we suffer?" How do we embrace an all-powerful and all-knowing God when we seem to be open game to the destructive powers of sickness, victims of interpersonal casualties, and finally death?

When these questions capture our thoughts, we are somewhat like the couple walking on the Emmaus Road in Luke 24. They were full of disappointment. They were a disillusioned couple without joy, without hope. For a while at least, they experienced what life would be like with God as they had walked with Christ prior to his crucifixion. Now, with heavy hearts they began to contemplate what the future would be like without Jesus. They were suffering. Proverbs tells us that "Hope deferred makes the heart sick, but a desire fulfilled is a tree of life" (Proverbs 13:12). What is interesting is that they were walking down the road of despair when Jesus joined them, and they began complaining to Jesus about...well, Jesus. They recounted how they had hoped Jesus would redeem them, but instead he had been crucified as a common thief, not the king they envisioned. Unfulfilled expectation regarding Jesus was the source of their "real life" pain and discouragement. The one they were walking with, Jesus, would turn out to be the key to turning their day around, they just needed to have reality explained to them. Doesn't that describe us on many days, when we don't feel as though God has been God for us? We need reality explained in a way that makes sense. The emptiness in our lives created by our neediness at every level leaves us with an unbalanced existence. Our time and resources are spent in avoiding suffering at all costs, and we devote little time to deeply contemplating the why or the meaning of suffering.

Just like the two men on Emmaus Road, in our own lives we complain *to* God *about* God. *I do not understand suffering, Lord.* Note what the Lord did when his disciples expressed this moral suffering of the heart, trying to figure out their loss. He began with the Old Testament and explained how the Messiah would enter into his glory through suffering. Jesus addressed their suffering by explaining his suffering. There is a huge lesson we can learn from this: *The way to endure our suffering is to understand Christ's suffering.*

Think about the suffering you have endured in your life. Think about what you may be going through right now. When it comes to experiencing a particular type of suffering, there is a direct relationship between how well you actually suffer and finding the meaning in your suffering. In other words, if we cannot attach meaning to our suffering, we run the risk of falling into despair. But if we can attach meaning to our suffering, if there is some value in what we are experiencing, we can endure anything.

Think about it: Nothing in life has meaning unless we attach meaning to it. This is especially true when it comes to language. Words mean nothing unless there is a common understanding and acceptance of the meaning we attach to a word. Take the word *ginormous*. Between 1948 and 1953 Americans started to blend two words *giant* and *enormous* together to communicate anything that was really giant or really enormous. At some point in time *ginormous* became a good word to communicate the meaning of something really big.[1]

Think about your own experience. What meaning have you attached to your suffering? Does the suffering you've experienced seem futile, just an unfortunate bump in your life journey? Maybe you feel more like that couple on the Emmaus Road. Do some situations make you feel hopeless or despairing? Do you have questions but no answers? There are so many reasons we suffer, and if we are unable to make sense of things, we are tempted to run from reality or self-medicate with alcohol or drugs. But if we can somehow find meaning in our suffering, everything looks different. Everything! That is what this book is about: how we can find meaning in our pain. How our less-than-ideal days on earth can say something really eternal.

Here's an example I shared with clients when I was a time-management trainer. It's an adaptation of the Franklin Quest time management training system. Imagine a steel beam one foot high, one foot wide, and twenty-five feet long. If I set that steel beam on the ground and told you I'd give you $100 if you would walk across it, you'd see this as easy money, since the top of the beam would only be twelve inches off the ground. But what if that twenty-five foot beam was two stories up between two buildings and I offered you a thousand dollars to walk across it? Would you do it then? The number of people that would agree to do it would go down dramatically. And if I took that beam and positioned it fifty stories up between two skyscrapers and offered ten million dollars if you would walk across it, only those who either have supernatural balance or no will to live might agree.

But what if I told you that your son or daughter was on the other side of that beam, and you would never see them again unless you walked across it, fifty stories above the ground. Would you walk that beam? In my seminars, almost every hand would go up. Yours probably would, too. Why? Because you suddenly have found a reason for walking across the beam— you've attached some meaning to it that just wasn't there before, even for ten million dollars. You'd walk across that beam to save your child, even if it meant putting yourself in great jeopardy or sudden death. For most people, their family represents a treasure that is worth suffering for if given the opportunity.

But the real question as it relates to this book is not whether you'd be willing to die instantly for someone you love, but whether you would be willing to die slowly for that person. As St. Paul said in 1 Corinthians 15:31, "I die daily." This can be a startling revelation for many of us. We would do our utmost to rescue a family member from a burning building or the raging sea, even if it meant losing our own life in the process—but dying slowly? Dying daily? That's something else entirely. I remember when my daughters were born. I felt such an intense love for them that each time I said to myself, "I would die for you." But the measure of my love was not that one time statement, but whether I would die slowly for them over many years.

In this book, I want to show you that there is meaning in your suffering. Life—real life! Suffering can take on a whole new meaning and all your suffering and discomfort can be seen from a much different perspective. A fascinating exercise is to think about the suffering you may be enduring right now and ask the question, "Does Jesus see this suffering as a waste or an opportunity?" In other words, do you think Jesus attaches meaning to your struggles? The answer is yes! Whether you are talking about giving up your life for a friend or driving to a wedding when you wanted to stay home, you can find meaning that will work for good in your life.

St. John Paul II is a good example of this type of daily dying. He lived with physical suffering and endured it courageously and publicly, right up to the end of his life. Although it would have been far easier to abandon his responsibilities and retreat from the public eye, he chose to demonstrate in a very transparent way what carrying one's cross daily means.

St. John Paul II was abundantly familiar with suffering. Looking back at his life, we note that he endured moral suffering at the loss of his entire family by the time he was twenty. As a young man Karol Wojtyla's life was not turning out the way he envisioned. It was less than an ideal life. He endured hard physical labor in stone quarries as a way to escape the Nazi regime. Even after he decided to become a priest, his seminary training was accompanied by the constant threat of government persecution.

Of course, young Karol Wojtyla would eventually be appointed Cardinal of Krakow and then ascend to the papacy in 1978. This courageous young pope who was familiar to theater, this man who knew the meaning of suffering would now stand on a world stage and demonstrate the meaning of both moral and physical suffering.[2]

The day after his election, John Paul II surprised everyone by leaving the Vatican for the Policlinico Gemelli, to make his first pastoral visit to Rome and Italy. He met with those who were sick with cancer and sat next to a friend, Andrej Maria Deskur, who was suffering from a stroke. It was reported that Cardinal Deskur would joke about being wheelchair bound; he said, "I am like the Coliseum, I'm a ruin, but very popular."[3]

Not only was St. John Paul II shot in Rome three years into his papacy, he also suffered physically from Parkinson's disease. Many will never forget the once vibrant and robust man struggling to stand and speak while looking out of his room at St. Peter's. I remember when he died. I went on the Geraldo Rivera show and said that we had just witnessed the greatest example of redemptive suffering in the modern age. Even though St. John Paul II couldn't speak well at all at the end, his life in those final days spoke very well. I remember thinking to myself, "I hope I can be that faithful to the end."

One wonders if Cardinal Deskur's statement about being like "a ruin, but very popular" stayed in the mind of St. John Paul II. Like the ancient Coliseum, St. John Paul II's life told a story of suffering well.

When it comes to pain and suffering, don't nurse it...or curse it...or rehearse it!

One thing you didn't see in the life of St. John Paul II was wallowing. Wallowing isn't a part of Jesus's plan for humanity either. Jesus didn't wallow in his suffering, and neither does he wallow in yours...he redeems it. In the same way that St. Paul tells us to make "the most of the time, because the days are evil" (Ephesians 5:16), we should say, "Make the most of your suffering, because the days are evil."

One of the ways you can "make the most of your time" is to keep your mind focused on the redemptive value of suffering and avoid falling into self-pity. Wallowing in meaningless pain only tends to prolong it—and it often exaggerates it. Repeatedly rehearsing or nursing family wounds creates distance between loved ones. Barriers to making amends are built when we focus on the interior pain brought on by betrayal or mean-spirited talk. Keeping your mind focused on the meaning of your suffering takes discipline and tenacity. Like the news reporter who fixates on pain and tragedy, so too does our mind tend to fixate on the headlines of pain in our heart. St. Paul once said, "We destroy arguments and every proud obstacle to the knowledge of God, and take every thought captive to obey Christ" (2 Corinthians 10:5). Part of finding meaning in suffering is related to capturing your thoughts and bringing them to Christ. Once you bring your suffering to Christ, you can look at it through a supernatural lens. Are your thoughts captive to the obedience of Christ, or are your thoughts out of control?

From Paralysis to Paradise

Michael Broitzman, a Bible student of mine, only missed three or four lessons over nearly a decade of classes. What makes him stand out in my mind is that Michael was a quadriplegic who could only move his face and neck muscles. When he was a young man, he was living a life bent on destruction. He struggled with alcohol, drugs, and wild parties. One evening he was walking on the edge of the road in a drunken stupor when a truck hit him. Paramedics said that his heart stopped several times, but he managed to survive. After it became apparent that Michael would live, the news that Michael would be completely paralyzed for the rest of his life was hard to hear.

His medical attendant challenged him to give his life to God. Michael was taken by her personal holiness and conviction, and he began to soften his heart to God. He accepted her challenge, and shortly after she accompanied him to several church meetings, he gave his heart to God. It was after he gave his life to Christ and understood the intimate union between Jesus and himself that the accident took on new meaning. Not only did he see the accident as a wake-up call, he began to understand the depth of participating with Christ's sufferings for the salvation of the world. Many times Michael told me that the night he was hit by the truck became the most valuable night of his life because it was that suffering that led to eternal salvation. For Michael, paralysis propelled him to paradise.

When Life Turns Upside Down

Fox News commentator Charles Krauthammer was in his first year of medical school at Harvard when suddenly he faced an unthinkable challenge. On a hot Boston day, Charles skipped class and joined some friends for a swim. You could say that it was an ideal day in his young and promising life. He dove into the swimming pool and hit his head on the bottom. He knew instantly that life had changed forever—he could not move his body and was motionless at the bottom of the pool. He dove into the pool with the same gusto that he dove into life with, but now it all stopped in a heartbeat.

Within hours he was upside down in a hospital bed. His whole life was upside down at this point. If this had happened to you, do you think you would have been able to take your thoughts captive, or would you have been captive by your thoughts? Charles didn't ask, "Why me?" or, "What if?" He didn't wallow in his suffering, nor did he stop living on that less-than-ideal day. Within weeks Charles resumed his medical studies at Harvard while lying flat on his back, reading his assignments with the help of an assistant. His professors even came to his room to repeat lectures. Charles Krauthammer graduated from medical school with his class, on time, and near the top of his class.

In 2007 Charles wrote an article for *The Washington Post* about Rick Ankiel, a Washington Nationals baseball pitcher who had a meltdown in the playoffs and couldn't throw a strike. For Rick Ankiel this brought on serious emotional turmoil. Charles reports in the article that Rick left pitching but returned later as a hitter. Charles put it well when he describes "the catastrophe that awaits everyone from a single false move, wrong turn, fatal encounter." He goes on to say, "Every life has such a moment. What distinguishes us is whether—and how—we ever come back."[4] Your chance of coming back victorious after tragedy is very much attached to whether or not you are able to find meaning.

Charles did not let his less than ideal day define who he was, but that fateful day did contribute to a fruitful career with meaning attached.[5] For Charles, the very head that crashed into the bottom of swimming pool became the head that would one day win the Pulitzer Prize! Your point of pain, too, can also result in a treasure you did not see coming! Start paying attention to that inner dialogue in your life, and resist the temptation to throw yourself a pity party. Tell the "wallows," the "what ifs," and the "if onlys" that the party has been cancelled.

Whatever you are going through right now, remember that God has a plan for you. He wants to be united to you so closely that it resembles a spousal relationship. As Christians, when we unite our suffering with Christ, when we take every thought captive to the obedience of Christ, we invite him to coauthor our lives and direct the narrative. We give ourselves over to Divine Providence, and we learn to trust the One who loved us enough to die for us. Even if our life narrative takes uncomfortable turns, we know that he knows the end of the story and the glory that awaits us if we share in his mission.

Throughout this book you will repeatedly be encouraged to do something with your suffering. By an act of your will, you can embrace the cross you are carrying. Taking your pain to the cross is taking your pain to the place of transformation. I remember the day Emily and I dropped off our daughter, Carly, for her first year at Franciscan University in Steubenville, Ohio. Dropping your child off at a college a thousand miles from home can be very difficult. The days turned to hours and the hours turned to minutes before we would drive away, leaving her alone for the first time in her life. Finally the time came, and I told her that I wanted to say good-bye at the foot of the big cross on campus. We walked to the cross, and it was there, at the foot of the cross, that I told her I wanted to leave her there because that is the place of transformation. Whatever she would later go through, whatever suffering she might encounter, the cross is the place where she would be transformed.

The moral suffering that comes from family, friends, and colleagues is often hidden in the heart but very painful. It's at the cross that we let it go; we die to self and allow God to transform us. Give it to Jesus. Offer it to him, by laying it at his feet—no, really, lay it down at his feet. Instead of reliving the pain, every time the thought comes to your mind, stop and see the Lord tenderly and lovingly waiting for you.

Perhaps he's sitting on a rock as a shepherd, overlooking his flock. He sees you walking toward him and gently smiles...and you take those thoughts and, like the Magi, lay them down as a gift at his feet. And it truly becomes a gift. You give Jesus your suffering. Bishop Fulton Sheen said in his book *Life Is Worth Living*, "Life may be like a game of cards; we cannot help the hand that is dealt us, but we can help the way we play it."[6]

"Offer it up..." We'll talk about that common phrase in more depth later in the book, but for now understand that the meaning in suffering is realized when we do something meaningful with it.

Chapter Three

BACK TO THE BEGINNING:
EVERY GENERATION HAS SUFFERED

Where and when did suffering originate? To answer this question, we must go all the way back to the book of Genesis and the story of Adam and Eve. God created Adam in his own image, after his likeness. Adam, equipped with reason, free will, and the capacity to love had great freedom in the Garden of Eden. God put Adam in charge of what we often call a paradise, caring for the garden and everything in it. Life was good—it appears to us modern people that Adam lived the ideal life seven days a week. There was only one major stipulation that God placed upon Adam:

> And the Lord God commanded the man, saying, "You may freely eat of every tree of the garden; but of the tree of the knowledge of good and evil you shall not eat, for in the day that you eat of it you shall die." (Genesis 2:16–17)

God knew that it was not good for Adam to be alone (see Genesis 2:18), so God created Eve to be his wife. Life became even more ideal for Adam. And then Satan appears on the scene.

Sometimes the story of Adam and Eve is discounted or not taken seriously because of the poetic literary style. It is true that the early story in Genesis is a poetic way of conveying the truth of our origins. Utilizing a powerful Hebraic style to tell us about our first parents is an engaging and useful way to communicate historical realities. Throughout the bible, writers will refer back to these key events to further explain why we are the way we are and how we can gain victory in our lives.

We commonly think of Satan appearing as a snake, but the Hebrew word used is *nahash*, which is rather ambiguous and has a variety of meanings. In addition to snake, the word *nahash* can also be used to refer to dragons and sea monsters (see Numbers 21:6–9 and Job 26:13). However, we know that this intruder was Satan and that he posed a real threat to Adam and Eve's ideal existence with God.

Satan begins a conversation with Eve. He tells her that eating a piece of fruit from that tree does not mean that she and Adam will die. Instead, he convinces her that it will instead make her and Adam like God, knowing good and evil. Eve succumbs and takes a bite of the forbidden fruit, and then offers it to Adam (who must have been right there throughout the entire conversation, completely silent).

Scott Hahn, in his classic book *A Father Who Keeps His Promises*, lists ten interesting underlying facts about this encounter.

1. Satan wanted Adam and Eve to die, spiritually if not physically.
2. Satan knew that he could not inflict spiritual death on Adam against Adam's will.

3. Adam and Eve dreaded death—they were aware of what God said would happen if they ate from the tree of the knowledge of good and evil.

4. God did not intend the Garden of Eden to be their final state. Heaven was to be their true home and their earthly life was meant to be a foretaste.

5. By giving him the command not to eat the fruit of the tree of the knowledge of good and evil, God placed Adam on probation, requiring him to exhibit some degree of self-denial.

6. Adam required more than simple self-denial to prove himself. It was necessary for Adam to engage in spiritual combat to deal with Satan. Satan knew this and would not give up easily. We know that, left to his own strength, Adam could not have been a match against Satan's wiles. Adam does not cry out to God in his distress.

9. Adam succumbed to pride and fell back upon his own resources, resulting in sin.

10. God the Father would not have forsaken his son in his hour of need if only Adam had cooperated with grace and called out to God for help. Either God would have empowered Adam to destroy the devil, or he would have accepted Adam's sacrificial offering of himself as a holy oblation, saving him from death and corruption and rewarding him with eternal glory in heaven.[1]

The main thing to keep in mind is that Adam and Eve sinned, and this "original sin," which is an abuse of freedom, resulted in death. They lost their trust in God and envy, which often comes from pride, entered into their lives. Because of sin, their reasoning faculties were darkened, their will was weakened, and they ended up in a state of concupiscence. Concupiscence is a disordered self-centeredness, a disordered desire for a thing, person or experience. Concupiscence resulted in a state of weakness and a tendency to sin. And as a result of our first parents' sin, suffering as we know it today was introduced into the world. Suddenly the harmony that existed between humans and God was gone. Furthermore, the harmony between Adam and Eve was damaged and so was the harmony between human beings and creation. The trust that was lost at the fall of mankind becomes a complexity of distrust both in our relationship with God and among our relationships with fellow human beings. Distrust threatens peace with God and each other. This lack of trust is the root of all sin, but it is also foundational in our relationship with God when it comes to understanding suffering.

You may ask, why is it that the original sin of our first parents so profoundly impacts our lives today? After all, we did nothing to warrant such a burden. The fact that each successive generation carries with them the evidence of original sin and concupiscence is indisputable. There has never been one super generation that seemed to miss the effects of Adam and Eve's sin. As the Apostle Paul said in Romans 3:23, "All have sinned and fall short of the glory of God."

The *Catechism of the Catholic Church* beautifully explains how both Adam's original holiness and justice were not for him alone, but for all of humanity. In the same way, Adam's sin affected the whole of our human nature and would transmit the fallen state from one generation to the next.

How did the sin of Adam become the sin of all his descendants? The whole human race is in Adam "as one body of one man." By this "unity of the human race" all men are implicated in Adam's sin, as all are implicated in Christ's justice. Still, the transmission of original sin is a mystery that we cannot fully understand. But we do know by Revelation that Adam had received original holiness and justice not for himself alone, but for all human nature. By yielding to the tempter, Adam and Eve committed a *personal sin*, but this sin affected the human nature that they would then transmit *in a fallen state*. It is a sin which will be transmitted by propagation to all mankind, that is, by the transmission of a human nature deprived of original holiness and justice. And that is why original sin is called "sin" only in an analogical sense: it is a sin "contracted" and not "committed"—a state and not an act. (CCC 404)

The good news is that there is a solution to the problem of this state of sin and future acts of sin and there is life after death. The *Catechism* puts it this way, "original sin is, so to speak, the 'reverse side' of the Good News" (CCC 389). The irony of it all is that suffering, which might seem like bad news, is part of the good news that works for the greater good. In addition, we will see that in Christ, the good news of the gospel involves suffering and makes sense of your suffering, as you will be invited to participate in God's amazing plan to restore humanity to himself through suffering.

When we look at the story of Adam and Eve, it might be hard for us to understand why the result of their disobedience was so radical: death and suffering for doing what? Eating a piece of fruit? However, when we look at the nature of sin, we see that the punishment was not simply for eating some forbidden fruit—their punishment had to do with the choice they made. The choice Adam and Eve made had tremendous results that ended in pain, and this is the same with you and me today. We are given the opportunity daily to make choices between good and evil, temporal or eternal, God's will or our will. Each of our decisions has temporal and potentially eternal consequences that affect us and can introduce us to compound suffering.

Three Things about the Tree

When we look at the "tree of the knowledge of good and evil" (Genesis 2:17), we see three things. The fruit tasted good, it was beautiful to look at, and it made one wise. We do not see the fruit possessing qualities that are indicative of sin in our own culture, such as bank robbery, murder or adultery. Instead, we are looking at three very good things relating to the fruit. What's not to like?

God gave Adam and Eve many good things to enjoy, but there was one good thing that was off limits. The battle was not a battle between something good and something bad; it was a battle between two good things. The one choice was God and the other was the fruit that God created. Simply put, the choice given Adam and Eve was the Creator or the creation.

St. Augustine can shed some light on this. In his *Confessions*[2] he talks about one individual sin at the age of sixteen that particularly bothered him a lot. That sin, ironically, happened to be related to a tree, a pear tree. Of all the things he could have listed that really bothered him, it was taking fruit from a pear tree. One day, he and his friends were walking down the road and they saw a common pear tree. They stole some of the pears, which they then threw at some pigs. And this bothered Augustine. He thought, "Why did I do that? Why did I do that?"

His first thought was, I did it just to be evil, for the simple thrill of stealing. But Augustine knew that good philosophy is the foundation of good theology, and so he corrected himself. He knew that we do not choose what we think is going to hurt us; we choose what we think will make us happy. When we sin, at its root is a choice we think will end up bringing us happiness. When St. Augustine looked at the episode with the pears, he thought, "I don't like pears; I didn't want the pears, really, so why did I do what I did?" His conclusion was that he did it because he wanted the camaraderie, companionship, and the acceptance of his friends. He was looking for acceptance and camaraderie, which are good things, but in the process he was disobedient.

Anything can become a source of sin if we choose the creation over the Creator. Whether it happens to be food, cars, hobbies, houses, education, or careers, anything you put before God can become sin in our lives. The pain and the suffering that come from sin are not always due to some big-ticket item like murder either. Simply putting any created thing before God, while it seems to promise happiness, ends up in unhappiness and ongoing emptiness. Oh, there may be an initial thrill in obtaining a thing, but it will never fulfill the place in our heart that we were hoping for. We are not created for things, and created things are not meant to fulfill us. True happiness and fulfillment only come when we embrace the Creator and walk according to his ways.

In the Garden of Eden, Adam and Eve were surrounded with a lot of good things. They had to make a choice between God and the one good thing he asked them not to indulge in, the fruit of the tree of the knowledge of good and evil. This is particularly poignant for Americans today, because America is so rich in good things. We have so much at our disposal—food, clothing, toys, gadgets, sports, and entertainment. There is rarely a thing or experience in our culture that we could not fulfill. Within a relatively short drive in the car or a walk down the road we can obtain nearly any created thing our heart desires. In a sense, we in America are surrounded by a Garden of Eden on steroids.

However, if you put created things before God, thinking they will make you happy, just the opposite can happen. What often results is unhappiness and suffering—what you thought was going to make you happy backfires. You thought that buying your dream house would make you happy, but you discovered that your happiness was fleeting. In fact, you might be wishing you could be out from underneath that dream house right about now. Instead of happiness, you feel overly burdened by all the expenses that came with the house, and how overextended you have become. Much of what we think will make us happy ends up becoming a trap and results in needless suffering for ourselves and our loved ones.

Archbishop Fulton Sheen once said, "The will that always insists on having its own way, begins to hate its own way. Those who live only for self, begin to hate self. Self is too narrow, confining and dark a sanctuary for happy adoration. Crosses are inescapable. Those who start with self-love have already created for themselves the possibility of millions of other crosses from those who live by the same pride."[3]

This is the nature of sin. This is the result of Adam and Eve's disobedience. In Genesis, we read how the punitive curse for Adam and Eve's sin resulted in pain and suffering and toil.

> To the woman [God] said,
> "I will greatly multiply your pain in childbearing;
>   in pain you shall bring forth children,
> yet your desire shall be for your husband,
>   and he shall rule over you."
> And to Adam he said,
> "Because you have listened to the voice of your wife,
>   and have eaten of the tree
> of which I commanded you,
>   'You shall not eat of it'
> cursed is the ground because of you;
>   in toil you shall eat of it all the days of your life;
> thorns and thistles it shall bring forth to you;
>   and you shall eat the plants of the field.
> In the sweat of your face
>   you shall eat bread
> till you return to the ground,
>   for out of it you were taken;
> you are dust, and to dust you shall return."
> (Genesis 3:16–19)

Adam and Eve's Suffering Is Reasonable and Remedial

The punishment God imposed on Adam and Eve was perfectly reasonable. And, while it resulted in pain and suffering, the pain they would go through as a result of the original sin would ultimately bear fruit. This is pure genius on God's part. The punishment for sin, the physical and moral results of the sin will act as a remedial experience that will produce fruit. God said to Eve in Genesis 3:16, "I will greatly multiply your pain in childbearing; in pain you shall bring forth children." Did you get that? Eve will be in pain, but the result will be a child. In other words, fruit shall emerge from suffering! In Hebrews 2:10 we see the same pattern in Christ. "For it was fitting that he, for whom and by whom all things exist, in bringing many sons to glory, should make the pioneer of their salvation perfect through suffering."

In the same way, Adam will sweat and work the ground, but the result will be a crop. Through this punitive suffering, they will learn to deny themselves, they will learn to suffer, and that suffering will result in fruitfulness. Therefore, we can see that their humble acceptance of that punitive suffering was actually remedial. God used it to teach them an important lesson on the relationship between love and suffering.

We shall see when we talk about the "last Adam" (Jesus) that the relationship between love and suffering is brought to a powerful new level.

There is some evidence in the Scriptures that the discourse between the serpent and Adam and Eve left them with the sense that they were being presented with an ominous veiled threat that suggested if they did not eat of the fruit of the tree there may be life threatening consequences.[4] This could explain why Adam was hesitant to engage the serpent or defend his wife, Eve. Whatever happened in Adam internally, we do know that the ordeal resulted in a fall due to pride and a distrust of God. The *Catechism* tells us "*hatred of God* comes from pride. It is contrary to love of God, whose goodness it denies, and whom it presumes to curse as the one who forbids sins and inflicts punishments" (CCC 2094).

The book of Genesis does not reveal to us what Adam and Eve's fate would have been if they had resisted the temptation of the serpent. If they would have suffered at the hands of the Serpent for obeying God, we do get a picture of the heart of the Father when we read about the death, burial, and resurrection of Christ. If Adam and Eve had understood this and had chosen to walk in love, God would have been faithful and acted on Adam and Eve's behalf in a life affirming way. At any rate, the result was suffering, a punitive suffering that had remedial benefits. It's as though God said, "Adam and Eve, you are going to learn to love." He wanted to teach them that love means being willing to suffer, even giving up your life if necessary.

As a result of the fall, original justice, the possession of sanctifying grace, was lost. Sanctifying grace is what makes the soul holy and gives the soul supernatural life. If someone dies without sanctifying grace in his or her soul, in other words they die spiritually. Because of mortal sin, they cannot enter eternal life with God in heaven. Adam and Eve committed spiritual suicide when they committed the original sin.

The good news is that God has a plan. This plan of sheer goodness was first announced immediately after Adam and Eve fell. Genesis 3:14–24 outlines the consequences of their sin and the first message of good news. Genesis 3:15 says, "I will put enmity between you and the woman, and between your seed and her seed; he shall bruise your head and you shall bruise his heel." At some point in the future the seed of the woman will crush the head of the serpent, but in the process of doing this the seed of the woman will suffer.

After God describes the remedial suffering that Adam and Eve would experience, Eve would give herself to her husband, resulting in pain at childbirth, and Adam would work the ground, experiencing the curse of thorns and thistles and sweat. While both would experience pain and suffering, both would result in fruit, a child and bread.

There is one important detail that can't be overlooked. In the Garden of Eden there were two very important trees. There was the tree of the knowledge of good and evil mentioned in Genesis 2:17 and the tree of life mentioned in Genesis 3:24. In their state of death, which was the result of committing the original sin, God blocked their access to the tree of life. Later, in the New Testament, we will see that as a result of God's supreme sacrifice of his Son, humankind will have the opportunity to receive sanctifying grace and will be given access to the tree of life once again. The tree of life is the cross, and the fruit of it is the Eucharist, the Body and Blood of the seed of the woman, Christ Jesus.

Suffering in Salvation History

St. John Paul II called the Scriptures "a great book about suffering."[5] Throughout salvation history, we see the people of God enduring suffering as a result of original sin, but we also see their suffering compounded by the choices they make.

Cain brutally kills his brother Abel, leaving Cain with a deep sense of moral suffering (see Genesis 4:8). We see God calling Abraham to be the leader of a new people—God's people. Immediately God instructs Abraham to leave his comfort zone, Ur of the Chaldeans. Jacob's sons betrayed their brother Joseph and sold him into painful slavery (see Genesis 37). Potiphar's wife lied about Joseph, resulting in Joseph being thrown into prison. The entire nation of Israel landed in Egypt where they were slaves for four hundred years (see Exodus 1). After the Exodus, Israel wandered in the desert for forty years due to the choice they made not to trust God in the taking of Canaan. The story of Job is synonymous with a life of suffering and asking why. In the story of Isaac and his sons, Esau and Jacob, we observe Jacob living a life of suffering. His deception results in having to flee from Esau, only to live in fear of him. His daughter, Dinah, is raped and experiences her own suffering. Much of Jacob's life could be described as reaping what he has sown. He fooled his father into giving him the blessing and then felt the suffering that came from being fooled by Laban when Leah replaced Rachael on the night of his wedding. Jacob suffered as a result of the behavior of his sons and it's reflected in the final blessings given to them in Genesis 49.

From King Saul to King David and throughout the difficult rule of King Solomon, people suffered greatly. Even the Psalter is filled with Psalms that convey the predicament of pain and suffering. Psalm 22:1–11 describes what would later be key to understanding the suffering of Christ.

> My God, my God, why have you forsaken me?
> Why are you so far from helping me, from the words
>   of my groaning?
> O my God, I cry by day, but you dost not answer;
>   and by night, but find no rest.
>
> Yet you are holy,
>   enthroned on the praises of Israel.
> In you our fathers trusted;
>   they trusted, and you delivered them.

To you they cried, and were saved;
  in you they trusted, and were not disappointed.

But I am a worm, and no man;
  scorned by men, and despised by the people.
All who see me mock at me,
  they make mouths at me, they wag their heads;
"He committed his cause to the LORD; let him deliver
  him,
let him rescue him, for he delights in him!"

Yet you are he who took me from the womb;
  you kept me safe upon my mother's breasts.
Upon you was I cast from my birth,
  and since my mother bore me you have been my God.
Be not far from me,
  for trouble is near
  and there is none to help.

Throughout salvation history, God uses suffering to capture his people's attention, and this suffering leads to repentance. As C.S. Lewis said, "God whispers in our pleasures, speaks in our conscience, but shouts in our pains; it is his megaphone to rouse a deaf world."[6]

As we work our way through salvation history, we observe many examples of human suffering. But we still haven't answered the question of how we can attach meaning to it. That's because, in order for us to understand our suffering, we must understand Christ's suffering. Before we look at the work of Christ as it relates to suffering, let's see the various purposes of suffering.

Chapter Four

Different Purposes for Suffering

As we look back at salvation history let's look at some well-known examples and how the stories bring out the many dimensions and purposes of human suffering. It is important to remember that most suffering involves a blend of several purposes. This helps, because no matter how you look at it, suffering is always a trial. No one enjoys suffering or seeks it out.

Punitive Suffering

One of the purposes for suffering that we see in salvation history is that it often served punitive purposes—suffering was the result of sin.

Punitive suffering has an educational aspect; it is valuable because it has a deeper purpose. St. John Paul II writes in *Salvifici Doloris*:

> In the sufferings inflicted by God upon the Chosen People there is included an invitation of his mercy, which corrects in order to lead to conversion.... Thus the personal dimension of punishment is affirmed.

According to this dimension, punishment has a meaning not only because it serves to repay the objective evil of the transgression with another evil, but first and foremost because it creates the possibility of rebuilding goodness in the subject who suffers.

This is an extremely important aspect of suffering. It is profoundly rooted in the entire Revelation of the Old and above all the New Covenant. Suffering must serve for conversion, that is, for the rebuilding of goodness in the subject, who can recognize the divine mercy in this call to repentance. The purpose of penance is to overcome evil, which under different forms lies dormant in man. Its purpose is also to strengthen goodness both in man himself and in his relationships with others and especially with God.[1]

This kind of suffering is disciplinary, but God our Father's punishment never stems from hatred—it is from love, for our good. In the same way, if you are a parent, when you have to punish your own children for misbehaving, it's not because you want to make them miserable, but to ultimately lead them to do good, resulting in a happy life. We experience this in our own lives. Every father wants to see his children happy and desires that they live well. The old saying is often true, "A father is as happy as his saddest child."

St. John Paul II uses the commonly recognized story of Job as "the most vivid expression" of punishment for wrongdoing as the explanation for suffering.[2] Job loses everything, his possessions, his sons and daughters, and finally he loses his health and becomes gravely ill. In the midst of this horrible situation, three old friends show up at the front door in an attempt to help Job find some solace in his pain. They try to convince Job that the only reasonable explanation for his spiraling life is he must have done something that would warrant this kind of punishment. Justice is what his friends appeal to in order to explain his tragedy. Certainly a just God will dole out punishment for wrongs done.

Certainly the Old Testament is filled with many examples that illustrate that if God's people sin, punishment and suffering will follow.

> See, I have set before you this day life and good, death and evil. If you obey the commandments of the Lord your God which I command you this day, by loving the Lord your God, by walking in his ways, and by keeping his commandments and his statutes and his ordinances, then you shall live and multiply, and the Lord your God will bless you in the land which you are entering to take possession of it. But if your heart turns away, and you will not hear, but are drawn away to worship other gods and serve them, I declare to you this day, that you shall perish; you shall not live long in the land which you are going over the Jordan to enter and possess. I call heaven and earth to witness against you this day, that I have set before you life and death, blessing and curse; therefore choose life, that you and your descendants may live. (Deuteronomy 30:15–19)

When Job was suffering, what Job's friends suggest "manifests a conviction also found in the moral conscience of humanity:

the objective moral order demands punishment for transgression, sin and crime."[3] While it is true that suffering has meaning as punishment when connected with sin, it is not true that all suffering is the consequences of a fault. In the story of Job, his friends were right in their understanding of suffering being the result of wrongdoing, but in Job's case the application was wrong. Job was blameless, leaving us with a mystery as to why he suffered so deeply as an innocent man. In Job's situation, his suffering appears to be a test, which was provoked by Satan, challenging Job's righteousness and fidelity.

There are of course other examples of suffering due to punishment in the Bible. In 2 Samuel 11 we see that David commits adultery with the wife of Uriah. After David arranged the death of Uriah on the battlefield, David was punished in chapter 12. David then went into the house of the Lord to worship. While David is broken as a result of his sin, the evidence of goodness being rebuilt in his life is found in Psalm 51.

> Have mercy on me, O God, according to your merciful
> love;
> according to your abundant mercy blot out my
> transgressions.
> Wash me thoroughly from my iniquity,
> and cleanse me from my sin!
>
> For I know my transgressions,
> and my sin is ever before me.
> Against you, you only, have I sinned,
> and done that which is evil in your sight.
> …
> Create in me a clean heart, O God,
> and put a new and right spirit within me.

Cast me not away from your presence,
and take not your holy Spirit from me.
Restore to me the joy of your salvation,
and uphold me with a willing spirit.
(Psalm 51:1–4, 10–12)

You see, the goal of suffering/punishment as a result of sin is to "create the possibility of rebuilding goodness in the subject who suffers."[4] St. John Paul II points out that this "is an extremely important aspect of suffering. It is profoundly rooted in the entire Revelation of the Old and above all the New Covenant. Suffering must serve for conversion, that is, for the rebuilding of goodness in the subject."[5] When one suffers as the result of punishment, the attitude should not be one of enduring and waiting until it all feels better. Rather, the one who suffers must focus on rebuilding the goodness that was lost due to evil.

I once knew a woman with a gambling problem. What happened to her illustrates the principle of suffering for the purpose of our conversion. This particular woman became addicted to playing the lottery. She spent so much money buying lottery tickets that she was unable to pay her bills. She always played the same numbers. One day she left her lottery tickets in her bedroom and then went out of town for the week. While she was away, the Powerball numbers were called, and she realized she had won several million dollars! Her excitement turned to dismay when she discovered that her mother, who lived with her, had cleaned her room and thrown out all the tickets.

She searched the garbage for those lottery stubs. She went to the city dump and searched everywhere. She called an attorney to see if there was any way she could prove that the winning numbers were hers. She did everything possible, to no avail. She finally realized that the suffering she was experiencing was meant to open her eyes to the extent of her gambling addiction and was meant to discipline her. Remarkably, she never gambled again.

A hard lesson, wouldn't you agree?

Probative Suffering

There is another kind of suffering in salvation history that could be called probative. We experience this type of suffering when we are being tested (think of the word *probation*). Job is a prime example in the Bible of probative suffering. His suffering took the form of a test. As we saw above, in a short amount of time, he lost all his possessions, his servants, his animals, even his sons and daughters. Next he himself became gravely ill. His wife's advice? "Curse God, and die" (Job 2:9). Through it all, though, Job does not assign this kind of meaning to his suffering. He knows that the suffering has come through God's hand somehow, but he continues to trust him.

In the end, God reproves Job's friends for their advice. Job's suffering is the suffering of someone who is innocent, and it must be accepted by faith; it is a mystery. When the period of testing was over, Job has a new understanding of who God is: "I had heard of you by the hearing of the ear, but now my eye sees you" (Job 42:5). Not only that, but God restored Job's fortunes by giving him twice as much as he had before, and he went on to have seven more sons and seven more daughters. "The Lord blessed the latter days of Job more than his beginning" (Job 42:12). Job's suffering had been a test, and he passed with flying colors.

Disciplinary Suffering

The third type of suffering is disciplinary, and like punitive suffering, it has an educational value. The sufferings inflicted by God upon the chosen people illustrate this time and time again. In every instance we see an invitation to God's mercy. He corrects the Israelites in order to lead them to conversion. Psalm 78 tells us that, in spite of all of God's miraculous provision, they sinned against him, testing him in their heart, demanding food, speaking against him, and disobeying his commands (see verses 12–20). The psalmist said, "When he slew them, they sought for him; they repented and sought him earnestly. They remembered that God was their rock, the Most High God their redeemer" (Psalm 78:34–35).

Scripture tells us that "Folly is bound up in the heart of a child, but the rod of discipline drives it far from him" (Proverbs 22:15). While the topic of spanking is controversial, the truth still remains. When folly is met with discipline, whether it be spanking or a privilege removed, folly is driven away.

The thought that God would allow suffering for his children may be hard for our modern minds to grasp. It was hard for people back in the Bible to grasp, too. When the soldiers of Antiochus Epiphanies came into Jerusalem in 168 B.C., they desecrated the temple and murdered many people. The Maccabees respond by saying:

> Now I beg those who read this book not to be depressed by such calamities, but to recognize that these punishments were designed not to destroy but to discipline our people. In fact, not to let the impious alone for long, but to punish them immediately, is a sign of great kindness.

For in the case of other nations the Lord waits patiently to punish them until they have reached the full measure of their sins; but he does not deal in this way with us, in order that he may not take vengeance on us afterward, when our sins have reached their height. Therefore he never withdraws his mercy from us. Although he disciplines us with calamities, he does not forsake his own people. (2 Maccabees 6:12–16)

God's intention was that his people would turn back to him, and he used disciplinary action to get their attention.

An important point to remember when pondering the discipline of the Lord is that this discipline comes from the heart of a good father; a father who loves his children deeply. Even when God reproves his people, he does not leave them but goes through the discipline with them. As a father, I know that my heart hurts along with my children when they are being disciplined. Proverbs 3:11–12 says, "My son, do not despise the Lord's discipline or be weary of his reproof, for the Lord reproves him whom he loves, as a father the son in whom he delights." Hebrews 12:4–11 echoes this truth, explaining that God disciplines us for our own good, in order to make us holy. And while that discipline is often painful, in the end the fruit it bears is peaceful and righteous.

The aim of godly discipline is a greater good, such as better decision-making skills or conduct that reflects holiness and character. Godly discipline should result in better choices in the life of the child. The application of appropriate consequences will hopefully result in words and deeds that will result in being formed more perfectly to Christ. Godly discipline should always leave a son or daughter with a sense of security rather than confusion.

Sometimes discipline seems harsh, but from God's perspective it is pure mercy. In the early Church there was an example of disciplinary suffering that comes to a man who was living a very immoral life. The hope was that his eternal life would be spared, but he would be turned over to Satan for the destruction of the flesh.

> It is actually reported that there is immorality among you, and of a kind that is not found even among pagans; for a man is living with his father's wife. And you are arrogant! Ought you not rather to mourn? Let him who has done this be removed from among you.
>
> For though absent in body I am present in spirit, and as if present, I have already pronounced judgment in the name of the Lord Jesus on the man who has done such a thing. When you are assembled, and my spirit is present, with the power of our Lord Jesus, you are to deliver this man to Satan for the destruction of the flesh, that his spirit may be saved in the day of the Lord Jesus. (1 Corinthians 5:1–5)

We are getting closer to learning how to attach meaning to all of our earthly suffering. Two of the most important truths are ahead of us: Jesus suffered for the sins of the world, and he actually changes our suffering by giving it meaning.

Chapter Five

SUPERNATURAL SUFFERING:
THE DIMENSION OF REDEMPTION

St. John Paul II gave us the key to understand the mystery of suffering. He said, "But in order to perceive the true answer to the 'why' of suffering, we must look to the revelation of divine love, the ultimate source of the meaning of everything that exists. Love is also the richest source of the meaning of suffering, which always remains a mystery: we are conscious of the insufficiency and inadequacy of our explanations."[1]

Our search for the meaning of suffering leads us to the subject of divine love. St. John Paul II tells us that divine love is the key to understanding the mystery of suffering. How many times do you watch TV shows, read books, consult with doctors, or attend seminars, and come away learning that the answer to the question of suffering is divine love? Divine love is rarely discussed when wrestling with the subject of moral and physical suffering. Most often we are disappointed with the popular answers to the why of suffering, but our need to know is great and we resurrect the search for answers after repeated bouts of discouragement. What is interesting is that the one Bible verse that most of us can quote from memory, John 3:16, is the very verse that contains the answer to the question of suffering. "For God so loved the world that he gave his only Son, that whoever believes in him should not perish but have eternal life." This single verse carries a truth that not only comforts those who are searching for love, but also offers a template for Christians for how to work with God in bringing salvation to the world. If we are to love those who are in our world, we must be prepared to give of ourselves, even to death.

Hear what St. John Paul II says: "Love is also the fullest source of the answer to the question of the meaning of suffering.... This answer has been given by God to man in the cross of Jesus Christ."[2]

If we are to truly understand suffering we must be willing to make an adjustment in our thinking and perspective. We must admit that ultimately the world and all the good things it contains will not satisfy the hearts cry for meaning. The answer belongs to a supernatural dimension. I would suggest that the longing of the heart as it relates to suffering is a natural cry for a supernatural answer. We must move to a new dimension, a supernatural dimension that goes beyond justice and provides the answers to the natural dimension of suffering. The supernatural dimension of suffering is the "dimension of Redemption."[3]

This supernatural dimension of divine love is found in the Trinity: Father, Son, and Holy Spirit. We see the supernatural dimension of suffering throughout salvation history. Salvation means liberation from evil, and salvation history is the record of God liberating humans from evil.

Three Ways to Know God
When it comes to understanding the questions of the heart and mind—who God is, who I am, what is right and what is

wrong—we are limited in our ability to arrive at ultimate truth. The *Catechism* tells us, however, that there are ways that we can come to know something of God.

> Created in God's image and called to know and love him, the person who seeks God discovers certain ways of coming to know him. These are also called proofs for the existence of God, not in the sense of proofs in the natural sciences, but rather in the sense of "converging and convincing arguments," which allow us to attain certainty about the truth.
>
> These "ways" of approaching God from creation have a twofold point of departure: the physical world and the human person. (CCC 31)

The World

First, you can look at the world around you, at the beauty and symmetry of creation and come to some knowledge of God as the origin and the end of the universe. St. Paul said, "For what can be known about God is plain to them, because God has shown it to them. Ever since the creation of the world his invisible nature, namely, his eternal power and deity, has been clearly perceived in the things that have been made. So they are without excuse" (Romans 1:19–20).

The Human Person

Secondly, the human person "with his openness to truth and beauty, his sense of moral goodness, his freedom and the voice of his conscience, with his longings for the infinite and for happiness, humans question themselves about God's existence. In all this he discerns signs of his spiritual soul. The soul, the 'seed of eternity we bear in ourselves, irreducible to the merely material,' can have its origin only in God" (CCC 33).

Reason

Third, utilizing reason, humans are capable of coming to a knowledge of the existence of a personal God. All three of these ways of coming to know something of God are limited. We can exhaust the beauty of creation, the complexities of the human person and the power of reason and still stand in need of further revelation to answer the questions of life, such as the meaning of suffering.

The *Catechism* tells us that "man stands in need of being enlightened by God's revelation, not only about those things that exceed his understanding, but also 'about those religious and moral truths which of themselves are not beyond the grasp of human reason, so that even in the present condition of the human race, they can be known by all men with ease, with firm certainty and with no admixture of error'" (CCC 38).

Once we come to the end of our natural ability to know about God, we need assistance, a deeper understanding. This order of understanding is called divine revelation. This revelation knowledge can only come with the assistance of God, in transmitting it, understanding it, and appropriating the revelation knowledge. In other words God has gone another step beyond natural means to supernaturally reveal in salvation history a deeper narrative to the meaning of life, and we are completely dependent upon him for this process.

It is only at this level of divine revelation that the meaning of suffering is fully understood. Not understood in the sense that I can now put up with life, but understood to the point where

I can now begin to live a full life with purpose whether I am comfortable or uncomfortable. Remember, if you cannot attach meaning to your suffering, you can fall into despair. But if God can reveal the meaning to you, and you attach that meaning to your circumstances, you can go through anything. Doesn't that sound empowering? You can go through anything if the meaning attached to your ordeal is big enough, deep enough, and eternal enough. This is where we are headed, so stay with me.

The Catholic Church teaches that divine revelation comes to us through three channels: the Bible, Tradition, and the Magisterium (the teaching authority of the Church). These three channels "are so linked and joined together that one cannot stand without the others."[4]

While all three are infallible, that is to say incapable of error, only the Bible is divinely inspired.

What do the words *inspired* and *inspiration* mean? The word *inspired* comes from the Greek word *theopneustos*, which means "God-breathed." When the Church speaks of the Bible as inspired, she means that the principal author of Scripture is God. *Dei Verbum* states it this way:

> For holy mother Church, relying on the belief of the Apostles (see John 20:31; 2 Timothy 3:16; 2 Peter 1:19–20, 3:15–16) holds that the books of both the Old and New Testaments in their entirety, with all their parts are sacred and canonical because written under the inspiration of the Holy Spirit, they have God as their author and have been handed on as such to the Church herself."[5]

The phrase "God is the author" is the classic formula used to describe inspiration, and it occurs in most of the official Church documents on biblical inspiration.

The apostle Paul describes how the principal author of Scripture, the Holy Spirit, made known the wisdom of God by communicating spiritual thoughts with spiritual words. Or as the New American Bible says, the Spirit was "describing spiritual realities in spiritual terms" (1 Corinthians 2:13). We must never stop marveling at how far God "has gone in adapting His language with thoughtful concern for our weak human nature."[6] He has stooped down to us like a father to his child and has adapted his thoughts to both our words and ability to understand. An important term to learn in relation to this subject of "inspiration" is "divine accommodation" or "condescension." Succinctly put, divine accommodation is the "adaptation and adjustment of the transcendent to the mundane."[7]

In other words, God is disclosing the wisdom of the ages in "baby talk." The Church trusts in the genius of the Holy Spirit as author to consign to writing (in a way we can understand) everything that God wanted written. This is what is meant when we say Scripture is inspired—it is written by the Holy Spirit.

Still more remarkable is the realization that God fully communicated his intentions while at the same time fully utilizing human authors. How did God do this? Clearly this is a mystery of faith, which cannot be completely understood in the natural.

When reading the Bible it is important to remember that words, people, and events describe a certain kind of history that is multilayered. In other words, when reading about the life of Israel in the Old Testament, there is a deeper hidden meaning, a truth that is realized in Christ. "As an old saying put it, the New Testament lies hidden in the Old and the Old Testament is unveiled in the New" (CCC 129).

Dr. Scott Hahn put it this way: "For God wrote the world the way men write books—to convey truth and love. Thus, nature and history are more than just created things—God fashions them as visible signs of other things, uncreated realities, which are eternal and invisible."[8] This is what makes the Bible so unique.

St. Thomas Aquinas quotes a formulation from Gregory the Great: "[Sacred Scripture] by the manner of its speech transcends every science, because in one and the same sentence, while it describes a fact, it reveals a mystery."[9] This means that the student and the listener must study and listen on multiple levels. In Bible study the student examines the facts and listen very carefully for the mystery that lies beneath the surface.

The human authors of the Old Testament revealed as much as they could, but they could not clearly share everything concerning the future and the fulfillment of God's plan. However, the Divine Author, the Holy Spirit could see the future and thus was able to tell of the saving work of Christ, from the beginning of Genesis on. All throughout the Old Testament we read about people and actions that describe the details of salvation history, but at the same time point us to a future action of Christ, and this is often related to suffering.

Isaiah describes a suffering servant that later will be fully realized in Christ:

> Surely he has borne our griefs
> and carried our sorrows;

yet we esteemed him stricken,
   struck down by God, and afflicted.
But he was wounded for our transgressions,
   he was bruised for our iniquities;
upon him was the chastisement that made us whole,
   and with his stripes we are healed.
All we like sheep have gone astray;
   we have turned every one to his own way;
and the Lord has laid on him
   the iniquity of us all.
He was oppressed, and he was afflicted,
   yet he opened not his mouth;
like a lamb that is led to the slaughter,
   and like a sheep that before its shearers is silent,
   so he opened not his mouth.
(Isaiah 53:4–7)

Later, in the New Testament, Caiaphas, the high priest prophesied about this suffering servant who would die for the people, saying "You do not understand that it is expedient for you that one man should die for the people, and that the whole nation should not perish" (John 11:50).

   Why did Jesus come to earth? To die for our sins, right? Yes... but what else? He came to suffer, die, and rise from the dead. He came to establish his kingdom, appoint his leadership, and communicate and impart his will to his Church. The gospel of Jesus Christ is not just about dying, which is where many people stop. He came to show us how to live, and in showing us how to live, he showed us how to suffer. If we really want an understanding of suffering, we need to look deeply into the life of Jesus.

One of the major keys to understanding Jesus is grasping the idea that his life is unquestionably and thoroughly tied to the words and deeds in the Old Testament. The words and deeds in the Old Testament contain a mystery, which is only understood when looking at the words and deeds of Christ. In other words, the entire Bible, whether New or Old Testament, is Christocentric. The entire canon of Scripture—all seventy-three books—find their ultimate meaning in Christ. If we can understand what Jesus was showing us through his suffering, we can come to understand our own suffering and the meaning behind it.

From the beginning of Matthew's Gospel through chapter 15, we don't see Jesus suffering; in fact, he does his best to avoid it at every turn, such as the time they wanted to throw him off the cliff in Nazareth (see Luke 4:29–30). But then, in Matthew 16, Jesus announces to his disciples that he will suffer, and he also tells them that he will die and rise again. This must have caught the disciples off guard; this wasn't the way they were envisioning things at all. Surely all of his work, his teachings and the time put into the formation of his disciples would not suddenly come to a crashing end? What meaning could this tragic end possibly yield if his movement was to continue on and prosper?

Peter thinks Jesus is mistaken. He is quick to say, "This shall never happen to you!" Perhaps Peter is concerned about Jesus dying under his watch as the new prime minister with the keys to the kingdom. And when Peter opposes Jesus's statement about his death, how does Jesus respond? He doesn't mince words, but rebukes Peter quickly (and rather harshly): "Get behind me, Satan."

Lost in Adam: Recovered in Christ

That response seems to be an echo back to the Garden of Eden. There the serpent tried to tell Adam and Eve that there was an easier way. The enemy said, "If you eat that fruit, you will not die. This will not be difficult. God knows that in the day you eat of it, you'll be like him, implying that He doesn't want you to become like him."

Notice how St. Paul draws the correlation between Old and New Testaments: "'The first man Adam became a living soul'; the last Adam became a life-giving spirit…. The first man was from the earth, a man of dust; the second man is from heaven" (1 Corinthians 15:45, 47). There is a tight connection between the actions of the first Adam and the corresponding actions of the last Adam, Jesus.

In the same way that the serpent suggested an alternative path, Peter says to Jesus, "God forbid, Lord! This shall never happen to you." But Jesus replies, "Get behind me, Satan!" (Matthew 16:22–23). And shortly after that Jesus makes the startling announcement in Matthew 17:22–23, "The Son of Man is going to be delivered into the hand of men, and they will kill him."

If we are going to discover the meaning of suffering and learn how to appropriate its benefits we must come face-to-face with the reality that many times our thoughts and ways are contrary to divine wisdom. This awareness and acknowledgement of our limited understanding will help us step forward into the realm of trusting God. It is our limited ability to understand God's grand scheme and our zealous attempts at self-preservation that keep us from accessing the treasure God wants to give us.

Isaiah said, "For my thoughts are not your thoughts, neither are your ways my ways, says the Lord. For as the heavens are higher than the earth, so are my ways higher than your ways and my thoughts than your thoughts" (Isaiah 55:8). We have to let go of our own understanding and allow the Holy Spirit to infuse us with a new perspective.

The ultimate expression of love is suffering to the point of death. St. Gianna Molla said, "One cannot love without suffering or suffer without loving."[10] St. John said, "Greater love has no man than this, that a man lay down his life for his friends" (John 15:13). So the ultimate moment of love comes at the time of death when we accept it for the greater good of another and turn it into a sacrificial gift of self. This is what Jesus did as an act of love for the world and we will see later that we are invited to join Jesus in this act of love. The *Catechism* tells us:

> *Death is transformed by Christ.* Jesus, the Son of God, also himself suffered the death that is part of the human condition. Yet, despite his anguish as he faced death, he accepted it in an act of complete and free submission to his Father's will. The obedience of Jesus has transformed the curse of death into a blessing. (CCC 1009)

Christ's whole life is a mystery of recapitulation. All Jesus did, said and suffered had as its aim restoring fallen man to his original vocation:

> When Christ became incarnate and was made man, he recapitulated in himself the long history of mankind and procured for us a "short cut" to salvation, so that what we had lost in Adam, that is, original justice,

sanctifying grace, we might recover in Christ Jesus. For this reason Christ experienced all the stages of life, thereby giving communion with God to all men. (CCC 518)

Jesus obtained an inheritance for us through his life, death, and resurrection. What was lost in Adam we have recovered in Christ, but it came through suffering. Your suffering can contribute to the recovery of life for others, too. This is where you can begin to find meaning when you suffer.

Jesus, by his suffering and death, took upon himself the curse of Adam. He paid the penalty of death for the broken covenant with Israel. The curse Adam encountered involved sweat, thorns, nakedness, and death. Jesus, as the second Adam, did what the first Adam failed to do—obey his Father and suffer for his bride. Let's look at the parallels.

Tested in a garden. The first Adam was tested in the Garden of Eden; Jesus, the second Adam, was tested in the Garden of Gethsemane.

Experienced sweat. The first Adam had to work by the sweat of his brow; in the Garden of Gethsemane, Jesus's sweat became like great drops of blood.

Encountered thorns. Where once the Garden of Eden was lovely, now it was full of thorns; Jesus had a crown of thorns put on his head.

Stripped naked. Adam realized his nakedness after the fall, and in the second Adam, Jesus is stripped naked before he was nailed to a tree and died.

These four parallels between the first Adam and the second Adam are very revealing. They show how the second Adam,

Jesus, takes upon himself the curse of Adam and Eve, and, by extension, the curse that covered all humanity due to original sin. He takes it upon himself by going through an ordeal that parallels what the first Adam went through. Hebrews 2:14–15 says, "Since therefore the children share in flesh and blood, he himself likewise partook of the same nature, that through death he might destroy him who has the power of death, that is the devil, and deliver all those who through fear of death were subject to lifelong bondage."

A Bride from the Side

In addition to the four parallels relating to a curse, there is a beautiful contrast between the first Adam and the last Adam in how they obtained a bride.

Adam experienced a deep sleep, and out of his side a bride was produced. After the last Adam, Jesus, died upon the cross—suffering the sleep of death for everyone, his side was pierced by a spear (see John 19:34). By his death he paid the penalty for humankind's sins (see 1 Corinthians 15:1–4), but at the same time something beautiful emerged—his Church, the bride of Christ. The *Catechism of the Catholic Church* puts it this way:

> The Church is born primarily of Christ's total self-giving for our salvation, anticipated in the institution of the Eucharist and fulfilled on the cross. "The origin and growth of the Church are symbolized by the blood and water which flowed from the open side of the crucified Jesus." "For it was from the side of Christ as he slept the sleep of death upon the cross that there came forth the 'wondrous sacrament of the whole Church.'"

> As Eve was formed from the sleeping Adam's side, so the Church was born from the pierced heart of Christ hanging dead on the cross. (CCC 766)

Jesus did what Adam should have done at the beginning. Hebrews 5:7–9 tells us that Jesus learned obedience through what he suffered, and thus he became the source of eternal salvation for all humankind.

God's love for the world absolutely involved suffering. When you really love someone, you are willing to pour yourself out; you are willing to give. Jesus poured himself out for the sins of every person who ever walked the face of the earth. He is "the expiation for our sins, and not for ours only but also for the sins of the whole world" (1 John 2:2).

When God loved the world he exercised his power with love and service. His expression of the Father's heart was demonstrated in both word and deed. Self-giving love is not something God does; it is who he is. We cannot separate God from selfless love that suffers, nor can we be afraid that he will suddenly change and become a tyrant. "God's almighty power is in no way arbitrary: 'In God, power, essence, will, intellect, wisdom, and justice are all identical. Nothing therefore can be in God's power which could not be in his just will or his wise intellect'" (CCC 271).

The Mystery of God's Apparent Powerlessness

The death of Jesus for our sins was not accomplished by a wave of the hand or a royal decree from a throne. He died for our sins by taking our place in time and space and received the punishment of death that was due all of us. "Faith in God the Father

Almighty can be put to the test by the experience of evil and suffering. God can sometimes seem to be absent and incapable of stopping evil. But in the most mysterious way God the Father has revealed his almighty power in the voluntary humiliation and Resurrection of his Son, by which he conquered evil" (CCC 272). The Scriptures tell us "all have sinned and fall short of the glory of God (Romans 3:23) and the "wages of sin is death" (Romans 6:23). This self-emptying of Jesus is the power of God in action. This is how his followers walk in power as well.

Once again, our thoughts and ways are very different from God's when it comes to the fruitfulness of suffering. The meaning of suffering became very real for one first century man by the name of Barabbas. The fact that Jesus died in place of us comes into clear focus when we see him standing alongside Barabbas before the Roman governor over Judea, Pontius Pilate. As was common practice, the governor would release one prisoner of the crowd's choosing. Pilate offered them a choice: Barabbas, a notorious prisoner, or Jesus. The crowd was adamant: free Barabbas and crucify Jesus (see Matthew 27:15–26).

A number of years ago when I was meditating on this portion of Scripture, suddenly I was struck with a sense of awe as I realized what was actually happening here before Pilate. Two men were standing together facing what looked like dark futures. Jesus, who is the pure, just, and merciful Son of God, stands before his accusers and Pilate. Barabbas, an insurrectionist and murderer who is worthy of death, also stands before Pilate. The juxtaposition of these two men is striking. Then I remembered that the meaning of the name *Barabbas* means "son of the father." Wow! Standing before Pilate were two sons of the

Father. One of them would be released, and the other would suffer certain death.

Who could have ever predicted that these two "sons of the father" would be tried together? By all rights the choice should be obvious, but then again our ways are not God's ways, and neither are our thoughts. Certainly Barabbas should be the one crucified, and Jesus released. What happened next, though, must have caused the heavens to shudder—Barabbas is released! The Son of the Father, the second person of the Trinity, was condemned to die a horrific death on a tree. How could this be? Doesn't Deuteronomy 21:23 say that one who hangs on a tree is cursed?

In God's wisdom and love, Jesus became a curse for you and me. Jesus takes on the curse, and Barabbas is released. What is truly amazing is that this natural replacement of Jesus for Barabbas is supernatural—it extends to you and me today. Jesus has released us from eternal death by his death on the cross.

The key to understand this unlikely switch is the word *released*. Barabbas was released and did not suffer death, but this was only because Jesus took his place, was held captive, and bore suffering and death on the cross.

Praise God that we are justified by his grace as a gift, through the redemption which is in Christ Jesus (see Romans 3:23). "For our sake he made him to be sin who knew no sin, so that in him we might become the righteousness of God" (2 Corinthians 5:21). You see, through suffering and the gift of self, Jesus paid the price for our sins, made it possible to become the righteousness of God, and gave us the power to become children of God (see John 1:12). Not only this, but we are raised to the dignity of "adopted children and thus heirs of his blessed life" (CCC 1).

We can rejoice in the fact that we have been delivered from the kingdom of darkness and welcomed into the kingdom of light, and we delight in the fact that we are friends with God. St. Paul put it this way: "If any one is in Christ, he is a new creation; the old has passed away, behold, the new has come" (2 Corinthians 5:17). To the Romans Paul said, "We know that *all things work together for good* to those who love God, to those who are called according to his purpose" (Romans 8:28, emphasis added). If all things are new, and all things work together for the good to those who love God and are called according to his purpose, "all things" must somehow include suffering. St. John Paul II proclaimed: "In the cross of Christ, not only is the redemption accomplished through suffering, *but also human suffering itself has been redeemed.*"[11]

Think about this amazing truth! Every bit of your suffering—from the pain of a headache or a broken arm to the loss of a loved one and even something as difficult as ALS—is redeemed. It was the precious blood of the Lamb of God that purchased you...*all of you*! When Christ redeemed you he received you back to himself. What God has purchased becomes very valuable and should not be looked upon as common or inconsequential. Therefore, your suffering is not inconsequential; it is extremely valuable in the economy of God. When you begin to agree with God and offer up your suffering, you begin to understand how the power of the cross makes all things new.

This chapter was packed with theology pertaining to the cross of Christ. It may have introduced some new concepts that you were previously not familiar with. When searching for the meaning of suffering—specifically your *own* suffering—it might seem easier to understand punitive, probative, and disciplinary suffering, but eventually you must progress from the natural to the supernatural. Truly understanding the meaning of your own suffering requires perceiving the supernatural dimension that goes beyond justice, testing, and learning. God takes us beyond our natural understanding and abilities into the realm of divine revelation. If you understand this truth, you see what many fail to see—you have begun to think with the mind of Christ (see 1 Corinthians 2:16).

Jesus came to earth to show us how to live, and in showing us how to live, he showed us how to suffer. He showed us that our suffering is meaningful. We can be confident that Jesus would not participate in and share with us something that was void of meaning.

It's only through faith that we can embrace God's mysterious ways and almighty power. Our weakness and suffering itself can draw Christ's power to us. We see this in the Virgin Mary, who thought nothing was impossible with God, and the *Catechism* says she is our "supreme model" (see CCC 273).

My friend, God has done great things for you, too. Have faith, and with total confidence say "yes" to Divine Providence.

Chapter Six

The Suffering Christ and Our Participation

Perhaps the biggest question we face, the one that stumps us the most, is this: "If Jesus suffered for me and released me from sin, then why should I have to experience anything he already went through? I thought Jesus said on the cross, 'It is finished!' Now I'm getting the idea that it's *not* finished—there is something expected from me in terms of suffering. Why?"

The quick answer is: "Yes, it is finished, but you, as the body of Christ, are contributing to it being finished." St. Paul not only speaks of completing what is lacking in the sufferings of Christ, but he even says he rejoices over this. Right about now you may be shaking your head and saying, "Am I missing something?"

We'll discover in this chapter that the mystery of suffering becomes even more complex and powerful as we begin to recognize the intimacy between the head, which is Christ, and his body, the Church. When we understand that the mission and method of the head is the mission and the method of the body, we will not be so quick to draw distinctions between the two. We might be very happy to let Jesus take the suffering and let us participate in the glory, but we will see that these two are never separated. Not only is the relationship of suffering and glory never separated, but neither is the head (Christ) and the body (Church). The head and the body work in union. First Corinthians 15:49 says: "Just as we have borne the image of the man of dust, we shall also bear the image of the man of heaven." That's why Paul could say, "For to me to live is Christ, and to die is gain" (Philippians 1:21).

The apostle Paul was very familiar with Christ's suffering. He was intimately aware of the powerful relationship between Christ's suffering and our suffering. In 2 Corinthians 1:3–7, Paul expressed it this way:

> Blessed be the God and Father of our Lord Jesus Christ, the Father of mercies and God of all comfort, who comforts us in all our affliction, so that we may be able to comfort those who are in any affliction, with the comfort with which we ourselves are comforted by God. For as we share abundantly in Christ's sufferings, so through Christ we share abundantly in comfort too. If we are afflicted, it is for your comfort and salvation; and if we are comforted, it is for your comfort, which you experience when you patiently endure the same sufferings that we suffer. Our hope for you is unshaken; for we know that as you share in our sufferings, you will also share in our comfort.

In Paul's remarkable message to the Corinthians, he points out that we, as the Church, share in both Christ's sufferings and his comfort. Paul goes on to explain that there is a real sharing in both suffering and comfort among the members of the Church. Paul encourages the Corinthian Christians by saying that they "share" in the suffering of Christ (see 1 Corinthians 10:7). The word *share* is the Greek word *koinnos*. The same root, *koinon*, describes the "communion" or "participation" we experience with Christ in the Eucharist (see 1 Corinthians 10:16).

St. Paul continues to draw his analogy in 1 Corinthians 12:12–13: "For just as the body is one and has many members, and all the members of the body, though many, are one body, so it is with Christ. For by one Spirit we were all baptized into one body—Jews or Greeks, slaves or free—and all were made to drink of one Spirit."

It was at the very beginning of St. Paul's conversion that he discovered the intimate link between Christ and Christ's mystical body. While on the road to Damascus to persecute Christians, "he fell to the ground and heard a voice saying to him, 'Saul, Saul, why do you persecute me?'" (Acts 9:4). Saul replied, "Who are you, Lord?" The answer came: "I am Jesus, whom you are persecuting" (v. 5)

St. Augustine describes the mystical union of head and body and how the sufferings of both the head and body are shared. If you persecute the Church, you persecute Christ. If the body suffers, the head (Christ) suffers as well:

> So whether I say head and body, or whether I say bride-groom and bride, you must understand the same thing. And that's why the same apostle, while he was still Saul, heard the words, "Saul, Saul, why are you persecuting me?" [Acts 9:4] because the body is joined to the head. And when as a preacher of Christ he was now suffering

from others what he had done himself as a persecutor, "that I may fill up," he said, "in my flesh what is lacking from the afflictions of Christ" [Colossians 1:24] thus showing that what he was suffering was part and parcel of the afflictions of Christ. This can't be understood of the head, which now in heaven is not suffering any such thing; but of the body, that is the church; the body, which with its head is the one Christ.[1]

Wasn't the suffering of Christ good enough to redeem the world? Yes, and it was good enough to transform our suffering into something of eternal value that participates in Christ's suffering. St. Augustine, like St. Paul, sees the sufferings of the body of Christ as part and parcel of the sufferings of Christ. The suffering of the Church is the suffering of the mystical body of Christ.

St. Paul develops this idea of sharing all things with Christ even further when he speaks of being completely conformed to the death of Christ and sharing in the power of the resurrection:

Indeed I count everything as loss because of the surpassing worth of knowing Christ Jesus my Lord. For his sake I have suffered the loss of all things, and count them as refuse, in order that I may gain Christ and be found in him, not having a righteousness of my own, based on law, but that which is through faith in Christ, the righteousness from God that depends on faith; that I may know him and the power of his resurrection, and may share his sufferings, becoming like him in his death, that if possible I may attain the resurrection from the dead. (Philippians 3:8–11)

St. Paul suffered the loss of all things in order that he might gain something. What is it that St. Paul longs to gain? He wants to share Christ's sufferings and become like him in his death in order that he might know Christ, the head, and the power of his resurrection. St. Paul considers everything a loss compared to the surpassing worth of knowing Christ Jesus. The *Catechism* describes the believer's union with the passion of Christ in the sacrament of the anointing of the sick.

> *Union with the passion of Christ.* By the grace of this sacrament the sick person receives the strength and the gift of uniting himself more closely to Christ's Passion: in a certain way he is *consecrated* to bear fruit by configuration to the Savior's redemptive Passion. Suffering, a consequence of original sin, acquires a new meaning; it becomes a participation in the saving work of Jesus (CCC 1521).

This puts the Christian in a very interesting position. Because we are joined to Christ as the body is to the head, we are united with him in our physical and moral suffering; our sufferings become one with his. In other words our suffering takes on meaning due to the mystical union that exists between the head and the body.

No doubt St. Paul was referring to the difficulties he faced at every turn. As the following text reveals, the suffering apostle experienced an abundance of physical and moral suffering.

> Are they servants of Christ? I am a better one—I am talking like a madman—with far greater labors, far more imprisonments, with countless beatings, and

often near death. Five times I have received at the hands of the Jews the forty lashes less one. Three times I have been beaten with rods; once I was stoned. Three times I have been shipwrecked; a night and a day I have been adrift at sea; on frequent journeys, in danger from rivers, danger from robbers, danger from my own people, danger from Gentiles, danger in the city, danger in the wilderness, danger at sea, danger from false brethren; in toil and hardship, through many a sleepless night, in hunger and thirst, often without food, in cold and exposure. And, apart from other things, there is the daily pressure upon me of my anxiety for all the churches. (2 Corinthians 11:23–28)

There was St. Paul, on his way to Damascus to inflict suffering on the Church. And then, once his eyes were opened and his heart given to the reality of Christ, his suffering was transformed into a counterforce that would bring down the kingdom of Satan.

The surprising thing to modern Christians is that, in the midst of all St. Paul endured, he found joy. What would your life be like if you could find joy in the midst of your less-than-ideal days? Would others notice? Would your children learn how to live in a new "dimension of redemption" as a result of observing you? Nehemiah records the activities of a crushed nation that was trying to rebuild after seventy years of exile. He reminds them, "The joy of the Lord is your strength" (Nehemiah 8:10). The joy of the Lord is a fuel that strengthens you in the midst of trials, and that joy acts as a supernatural billboard that attracts others.

St. Paul didn't have the corner on the "suffering can lead to joy" market. St. James tells us, "Count it all joy, my brethren, when you meet various trials" (James 1:2). Again, why would we count it all joy? Because we know that our suffering is in union with Christ; it has value and meaning, and it gives us the opportunity to love as Christ loves.

In the 1981 blockbuster movie *Chariots of Fire*, a story is told about two young British sprinters competing for honor in the 1924 Olympics. Harold Abrahams, who was Jewish, runs to raise his status in the Cambridge society. Eric Liddell, born of Scottish missionaries, is a Christian and runs because he believes it pleases God. At the heart of Eric's motivation to run is his desire to honor and glorify the Lord. He says, "I believe God made me for a purpose, but he also made me fast. And when I run, I feel His pleasure."[2]

In the same way, God made us to love, and when we love, we feel his pleasure. We can actually know the heart of God, and if we are truly in union with him, we can feel his pleasure. When we divest ourselves of our insistence upon our own will and desires and give ourselves to others in love, we truly become who we were created to be, and we experience our true vocation as sons and daughters of God. We are not put on earth primarily to possess things and focus on personal achievement. We are put on earth to love and serve God with the hope of being with him in heaven forever. This is our reward, and to achieve it, we must become small.

To Love Big, We Must Become Small

The story of the Good Samaritan is the classic tale of a man who traveled from Jerusalem to Jericho and fell among thieves. He was beaten, robbed, and left for dead. The highlight of the story is the kindness of an unlikely man, a Samaritan, who cares for the suffering man on the side of the road. It isn't the fact that it was a *Samaritan* who helped the abandoned man, although there is a beautiful message in that. It isn't the fact that the Samaritan *helped* the man that catches our attention. It was the *way* he did it. He demonstrated the complete self-giving that Jesus emphasized. He didn't give and then stop—it was open-ended giving, with no end in sight.

For Jesus, what constitutes love is not giving out of surplus, but giving in a way that expends oneself, emptying oneself for others, like the widow giving her last mite (see Luke 21:1–4). This is self-emptying is also described as "turning the other cheek" (Matthew 5:39); "walking the second mile" (Matthew 5:41); giving up your cloak in addition to your coat (see Matthew 5:40), and ultimately laying your life down for a friend (see John 15:13). Jesus said, "If any man would come after me, let him deny himself and take up his cross daily and follow me. For whoever would save his life will lose it; and whoever loses his life for my sake, he will save it" (Luke 9:23–24).

When we read those words, the tendency is to think that if you give of yourself and empty your life, you will have found a way of gaining something more for yourself. This is not true! We don't empty ourselves to gain something for ourselves; we empty ourselves because that is love, and we are created in the image and likeness of God, who is love. The Trinity is an exchange of love, and we are called to participate in that exchange by yielding ourselves to God in service. We need no other reward, because the reward is loving. Loving is life itself, and love is what we are called to do. Do you see now why St. Paul said, "For the word of the cross is folly to those who are perishing, but to us who are being saved it is the power of God" (1 Corinthians 1:18)?

Jesus explains to his disciples that the key to fruitfulness is dying. He said, "Truly, truly, I say to you, unless a grain of wheat falls into the earth and dies, it remains alone; but if it dies, it bears much fruit. He who loves his life loses it, and he who hates his life in this world will keep it for eternal life" (John 12:24–25).

We have a choice to make in life. Do we truly believe that Jesus is "the way, and the truth, and the life" (John 14:6)? If we do, then we must live our lives like he lived his, offering ourselves up for the greater good of others. St. John even gives us a way to measure whether we are living in life or abiding in death. "We know that we have passed out of death into life, because we love the brethren. He who does not love remains in death" (1 John 3:14).

We must completely reorient our lives to loving—even in our suffering—and heed Jesus's new commandment that we love one another the way he has loved us (see John 15:12). It's important to remember, that Jesus, in his suffering and death, is not merely giving a demonstration of what love would look like—he is actually God on earth loving in real time. What is paradoxically strange to the world's way of thinking becomes the model of living for the Church. The longer you walk with Christ, the more you will start seeing his worldview as normal and desirable. You'll come to be, like him, "one who serves" (Luke 22:27).

The mission and experience of the head is the mission and experience of the body. In other words, Jesus's mission to redeem the world is also the mission of the body of Christ, the Church. If the body of Christ is busy avoiding a sacrificial life, the work of God in the world will be divided. As part of Christ's body, our mission is to redeem the world; our experience is Christ's experience. This requires us to live in harmony with God's will and conform every aspect of our lives to Christ.

Two Different Views of the Relationship of Head and Body

While the teachings of the Catholic Church on redemptive suffering can be difficult for us as Catholics to understand, they are especially difficult for many Protestants. It's tempting to claim all the comfortable aspects of being associated with Christ, while assigning Jesus the more difficult and painful aspects of redemption.

There are two ways of looking at the relationship between the head (Christ) and the body (the Church) as it pertains to suffering. The first one—which is not found in the Bible—is that Jesus simply did everything for us. He suffered for us, he redeemed us, he intercedes for us, he shepherds us, he heals us, he guides us, he prospers us—he does everything, and all we do as the body of Christ is receive the benefits. In this very modern gospel, our part is to receive the benefits of this covenant relationship. This is a very popular view in America today—we might call it the "American Gospel." It leads to erroneously basing one's spiritual maturity on physical rewards. The more faith you have, the more comfortable and pain-free you will be.

While there are physical rewards in the Old Testament, when we come to the New Testament we see that the reward is not gold and silver but Christ himself. This is why Peter said to a lame man at the gate of the temple "I have no silver and gold, but I give you what I have; in the name of Jesus Christ of Nazareth, walk" (Acts 3:6). What did Peter have? Peter had Jesus to give to the man, which is better than silver or gold.

This one-sided look at being the body of Christ is not the biblical view of head and body participation. As Catholics, we also believe that Jesus suffered for us. He died for us. He arose from the dead. He taught us. He healed us. He counseled us. He supplies our needs. Yes, he did everything. But as a master builder, as one who understands the intimate connection between himself and his Church, he has chosen to share his mission with us. He tells us:

> If the world hates you, know that it has hated me before it hated you. If you were of the world, the world would love its own; but because you are not of the world, but I chose you out of the world, therefore the world hates you. Remember the word that I said to you, "A servant is not greater than his master." If they persecuted me, they will persecute you. (John 15:18–20)

Unity in Mission

The second way of looking at the relationship between the head (Christ) and the body (the Church) as it pertains to suffering is unity in mission. If our mission is the same as the mission of the Messiah, what does that mean for us? We know that Christ is the intercessor. Paul tells Timothy, "For there is one God, and there is one mediator between God and men, the man Christ Jesus, who gave himself as a ransom for all" (1 Timothy 2:5–6). This sounds as if there is *only one* intercessor. But this Intercessor shares his intercessory role with us when he says, "But I say to you, Love your enemies and pray for those who persecute you" (Matthew 5:44). Jesus is the healer, but he shares his healing mission with us by telling us that his disciples "will lay their hands on the sick, and they will recover" (Mark 16:18). God is our Father, but he gives us spiritual fathers here on earth to share in his fatherly mission. St. Paul said, "For though you have countless guides in Christ, you do not have many fathers. For I became your father in Christ Jesus through the gospel" (1 Corinthians 4:15).

Christ suffered for the sins of the world—no one would dispute this. But listen to how Paul unlocks the mystery of the union between the body of Christ and the head when he says, "Now I rejoice in my sufferings for your sake, and in my flesh I complete what is lacking in Christ's afflictions for the sake of his body, that is, the Church" (Colossians 1:24). In this verse, Paul reveals the mystery of the intimate connection between the body and the head. Yes, Jesus suffered for the sins of the world, but as in all areas of his mission, he shares his life with us.

What Do We Gain By Suffering with Christ?
Why would Jesus invite us to share in his sufferings? What could possibly be lacking in the sufferings of Christ? What could Paul have meant when he wrote, "In my flesh I complete what is lacking in Christ's afflictions" (Colossians 1:24)?

When Jesus rose from the dead, did he suddenly realize that he had only suffered 97 percent of the 100 percent necessary for the redemption of humanity? Is there a chance that a certain percentage was left unfulfilled by some heavenly mistake or oversight? We know that can't be the case.

As stated earlier in this book, St. Augustine wrestled with this question of sharing in the sufferings of Christ. His answer was that what is lacking is the sufferings of the mystical body of Christ, the Church—implying that there is a role for us to play in the sufferings of Christ.

St. John Paul II examined this whole issue of sharing in Christ's sufferings in *Salvifici Doloris*. His conclusion was that nothing was lacking in Christ's sufferings, but so that we might know the love of God more deeply, Christ has made room in his suffering for us to participate in it. John Paul II put it this way:

> The Redeemer suffered in place of man and for man. Every man has his own share in the Redemption. Each one is also called to share in that suffering through which the Redemption was accomplished. He is called to share in that suffering through which all human suffering has also been redeemed. In bringing about the Redemption through suffering, Christ has also raised human suffering to the level of the Redemption. Thus each man, in his suffering, can also become a sharer in the redemptive suffering of Christ.
>
> This discovery caused Saint Paul to write particularly strong words in the Letter to the Galatians: "I have been crucified with Christ, it is no longer I who live, but Christ who lives in me: and the life I now live in the flesh I live by faith in the Son of God, who loved me and gave himself for me" (Gal 2:20). Faith enables the author of these words to know that love which led Christ to the Cross. And if he loved us in this way, suffering and dying, then with this suffering and death of his he

lives in the one whom he loved in this way; he lives in the man: in Paul. And living in him—to the degree that Paul, conscious of this through faith, responds to his love with love—Christ also becomes in a particular way united to the man, to Paul, through the Cross. This union caused Paul to write, in the same Letter to the Galatians, other words as well, no less strong: "But far be it from me to glory except in the Cross of our Lord Jesus Christ, by which the world has been crucified to me, and I to the world" (Gal 6:14).[3]

Why does the Heavenly Father want you to participate in the suffering that Christ went through for the world? The answer is that he wants you to know what love is. He wants you to know how to love, and he knows that suffering can teach you this. This is where Adam and Eve failed, and this is where so many fail today—they avoid suffering at all costs, because it involves pain and sacrifice. The key to understanding this issue of what is lacking in the sufferings in Christ, the key to understanding the relationship between the head and the body of Christ, can be summed up in one word: sharers. You and I are sharers in Christ's suffering. He is sharing this opportunity with us. We are participating with him.

That's why Paul can say that he completes what is lacking in Christ's afflictions. Paul understood that the suffering he was going through somehow allowed him to share in Christ's suffering for the world. And lest you think Paul was some kind of glutton for pain, he was just as human as the rest of us. In his own life, there was a time when he asked the Lord three times to remove a particular suffering from him (see 2 Corinthians

12:8). The response he received from the Lord was *not*, "Oh, my oversight. That's right, I took care of all that suffering. You don't have to do anything." No, God's response was, "[Paul], my grace is sufficient for you, for power is made perfect in weakness" (2 Corinthians 12:9).

Paul further explains that not only do we participate in Christ's sufferings—the weaknesses we experience are actually opportunities for power to be perfected in us. It is completely opposite of the way the world thinks. Think about it. What looked like the worst thing that ever happened on earth—Christ hanging on a cross, bleeding to death—became the source of salvation for the entire world. The point of weakness became the point of strength; it was transformed into the power over death and Hell. We have to get it through our heads that the kingdom of God is an upside-down kingdom according to the world's perspective. Weakness confounds the wise. The poor and obscure confound the rich and famous. Remember your less-than-ideal day? That less-than-ideal day can be transformed as well.

St Paul says it this way:

> We are afflicted in every way, but not crushed; perplexed, but not driven to despair; persecuted, but not forsaken; struck down, but not destroyed; always carrying in the body the death of Jesus, so that the life of Jesus may also be manifest in our bodies. For while we live we are always being given up to death for Jesus' sake, so that the life of Jesus may be manifested in our mortal flesh.... We speak, knowing that he who raised the Lord Jesus will raise us also with Jesus. (2 Corinthians 4:8–11, 14)

Paul understood the mystery of union with Christ. Christ not only redeemed our souls from death and hell, he redeems our suffering, too. That means that when you are in union with Christ and you offer up your suffering in union with him, your suffering is redeemed. You are valuable—so valuable that Christ wanted to redeem even your suffering and make it meaningful in your life. Our suffering united to Christ trumps any less-than-ideal day. In Christ, all of life has meaning now. We have the opportunity to participate in the redemption of the world by offering up our suffering in union with Christ, and there is a treasure trove of meaning for us to uncover!

Chapter Seven

WHAT ABOUT YOU?
READY TO OFFER IT UP?

Now that we've touched on the meaning of suffering, let's look at some of the practical ways you can offer your suffering in union with Christ.

You can now face your suffering, from your less-than-ideal days to serious affliction, knowing that God's grace is sufficient for you. There is a sense of consolation in knowing that your trials are part of the finished work of Christ. Grace is the life of the Trinity, and the life of the Trinity is what sustains you in difficulties. Christ's life in you is sufficient, and his power is perfected in weakness. You might say you feel weak, but he answers, "Come to me, all who labor and are heavy laden, and I will give you rest. Take my yoke upon you, and learn from me… and you will find rest for your souls" (Matthew 11:28–29).

What does it mean to take Christ's yoke upon you? This phrase was actually a common phrase that rabbis would say when summoning disciples to be faithful followers. It means embracing Jesus's worldview, his mission, and the methods he used to carry out that mission. To take his yoke upon you also involves being open and willing to offer up your suffering—whatever that is—for the redemption of the world. You become a partner with Christ, carrying out his wishes and will. You are participating with him in his mission.

I remember when I was a kid and my friends would play whiffle ball on Saturday mornings. Sometimes my dad had other plans for my Saturday mornings, such as when he enlisted my help in building wooden steps leading up to our house or when he called me to help lay bricks down to build a new patio. I didn't want to spend Saturday mornings working with my dad while my friends were playing ball; to me it sure seemed like a form of suffering. My dad taught me how to measure boards, how to cut them and nail them, and so forth, even though I really had no interest in doing any of it. But now I look back, and see the wisdom of my father who asked me to "participate in his will" for our yard. He wanted me to spend time with him, and it was during those times of working with my dad that I got to know him better and love him more. I knew his heart; I knew what he wanted. I could have read about building wooden steps in a book, which I probably would have forgotten, but instead he said, "Work with me. Do what I am doing."

It is very similar in the kingdom of God. We can read about suffering all we want. We can watch Catholic TV, listen to Catholic radio, and read Catholic books, but we will soon realize that suffering cannot be taught in the abstract. Suffering is raised to the level of a vocation: "Come follow me." In other words, you will only experience this mystery of Christ if you actually participate with him by uniting your suffering to his, both physically and morally. In light of the passion of Christ, all human suffering takes on new light. If we are crucified with Christ, we are one with him; we are crucified with him, we rise from the dead with him in baptism, and now we continue to carry out his mission in the same way he carried it out. In union with him, we do our part—we teach, we offer up our suffering, we love. This is filling up Christ's sufferings.

Human Suffering Elevated

In bringing about the redemption through suffering, Christ has also raised human suffering to the level of redemption. Thus, each of us can become a sharer in the redemptive suffering of Christ through our individual sufferings. An example of this occurred when Jesus was carrying his cross on the way to Calvary. In Mark 15:21, Simon the Cyrene was passing by, and the soldiers compelled him to help Jesus carry the cross. This was a foreshadowing of our calling to pick up our crosses. Jesus says in Luke 9:23, "If any man would come after me, let him deny himself and take up his cross daily and follow me." Simon may not have planned to carry a cross that day, but as the circumstances played out he found himself participating in the most important cross of all time. The cross of Jesus became Simon's cross in an instant. What may have begun as an ideal day for Simon, suddenly became a less than ideal day, but due to his decision to embrace the cross rather than reject it, that day became his best day ever.

Paul said in 2 Corinthians 1:5, "For as we share abundantly in Christ's sufferings, so through Christ we share abundantly in comfort too." This is a fantastic promise for us! When we suffer, we can be certain that we will be comforted abundantly. Paul taught that it was imperative that we suffer if we want to share in Christ's glory. In Romans 8:17, he said, "We are children of God, and if children, then heirs, heirs of God and fellow heirs with Christ, provided we suffer with him in order that we may also be glorified with him." Paul goes on to say, "I consider that the sufferings of this present time are not worth comparing with the glory that is to be revealed to us" (Romans 8:18). Paul argues that this is the reason we don't lose heart. "For this slight momentary affliction is preparing for us an eternal weight of glory beyond all comparison, because we look not to the things that are seen, but to the things that are unseen" (2 Corinthians 4:17–18).

St. Thérèse of Lisieux understood the honor and mystery of suffering with Christ at a very young age. Recalling her First Communion, she said, "I felt born within my heart a *great desire to suffer*.... [Suffering] had charms about it which ravished me without my understanding them very well. Up until this time, I had suffered without *loving* suffering, but since this day I felt a real love for it."[1]

So now, just as Adam bore fruit in the natural, we now bear supernatural fruit through our suffering. That's why Peter could say, "Rejoice insofar as you share Christ's sufferings, that you may also rejoice and be glad when his glory is revealed" (1 Peter 4:13).

In paragraph 27 of *Salvifici Doloris*, John Paul II gives us in a very concise way a look at our participation with Christ when we offer up our sufferings with him. He says,

> The springs of divine power gush forth precisely in the midst of human weakness. Those who share in the sufferings of Christ preserve in their own sufferings

a very special particle of the infinity treasure of the world's redemption and can share this treasure with others."[2]

Now, that tells us something very, very powerful: Sharing in the sufferings of Christ involves an act of your will. It's saying, "Yes, I will offer up my suffering in union with the sufferings of Christ." St. John Paul says that if you do that, if you offer up your suffering, you are going to share a very special particle in bringing about the world's redemption. You have a part to play, and it's a treasure that you can share with others. That means that through your sufferings you can pray for your family. You can offer up your suffering for the pope, or for the president, or for your priest, or for your daughter, or for others you know who are sick. Through your sufferings, you can actually love the way Christ loves, and you are not limited by distance or time.

I like to call suffering "heavenly cash," available for you to spend on loved ones. Marguerite Duportal calls suffering a "marvelous coin" that purchases what cannot be bought.[3] If you think your suffering is useless, you are missing the point. Your suffering isn't supposed to be meaningless—it's meant to be united with Christ's suffering, thereby invested with value. Your suffering provides you with an incredible opportunity to work with him in redeeming the world, and it is an incredible opportunity to love the way he loves. I've seen this happen in my own life, as well as countless others around the world. Marguerite Duportal explains this idea of suffering as true wealth:

In the sacred commerce that God permits a soul to carry on with Him, pain acquires a value of the highest order, in fact becomes the noblest of values. Suffering becomes a power. Those who suffer, those who are afflicted are the really wealthy people of this world. They are rich, but frequently they do not know how to spend it.[4]

A Pain in the Neck

In my early forties, I struggled with tremendous pain. I noticed one night at dinner that when I reached across the table for the salt, a lightning flash went down my left arm. From that day on I began to experience excruciating pain in my neck and arm, which continued for days, and then weeks. Finally I made an appointment to see the doctor, thinking I might have a pinched nerve. The doctor diagnosed me as having a bulging disk in my neck. He prescribed a treatment regime, which consisted of a series of shots and specific exercises and stretching.

In spite of all this, nothing seemed to help. The pain went on for more than nine months. During this time I started to study more about the whole issue of pain and the meaning of suffering. I remember talking regularly on the phone with my dear friend, Scott Hahn, about the topic of suffering and how to respond to it. By that time, I knew intellectually I was supposed to offer it up in union with Christ, but in all honesty it was still an abstract idea. I had no clue as to how I was to actually offer it up. I was frustrated, and this added to the emotional toll, as unrelenting physical pain so often wears one down. The pain was so intense that I was on the verge of despair.

Eventually I required emergency surgery, which entailed having my neck fused. The doctor explained to me that my C6-7 disk in my neck had split and if I did not have surgery immediately, I could lose considerable muscle control in my left arm. He went on to explain that they would take out the broken disk and replace it with a bone fashioned from my left hip. The whole thing was quite an ordeal, and I must confess that I was not always proud of how I handled the pain.

To be honest with you, I don't think that men are great at suffering. I think women tend to suffer more valiantly than men, while men have a tendency to be babies. We sit down in our La-Z-Boy chair with our sore back and ask the kids to bring the remote to us; we ask our wife to bring us a beer so we can relax. We put everyone on notice, in effect saying: "I will not be a functioning father or husband for the next month."

Case in point: One night I couldn't sleep, so I went downstairs. And I just started crying. I said to myself, "I can't take this anymore. I can't take this pain in my body anymore, and I'm emotionally drained from lack of sleep." I cried out to the Lord, asking him in a straightforward manner, "How do I offer this up?" I actually raised my voice in desperation. "How do I offer it up? What do I do? I know the theological meaning of suffering, but I do not know how to do this. I do not know how to do it practically."

And then suddenly, the answer came. (I'll give you a hint: A certain shoe company later "borrowed" it from me.) *Just do it!* The answer to my prayers was easier than I thought. You know, sometimes we make things so much more complicated than we need to make them.

And so I just did it. I prayed, "Lord, I offer up this horrible pain in my neck in union with your suffering on the cross. Make it redemptive and use it for your purposes." Later in this book I'll continue with this story and explain what happened next.

I'll give you a clue—I applied my "particle" of suffering for my daughter in an amazing way.

Offer It Up

"Just offer it up." Some of us grew up hearing this phrase from our Catholic parents. Even if we heard that phrase repeatedly, we most likely didn't understand fully what it meant. Certainly this is a foreign phrase to our Protestant brothers and sisters. It sounds strange—after all, what does God want with my broken arm or seven stiches in my knee?

In the midst of our pain and suffering, we really have two choices. We can draw attention to ourselves, or we can exercise our will and offer our suffering to Christ to use for his purposes. Many times we end up focusing on ourselves in our weakness, hoping for sympathy, relief—anything to make us feel better. Doing this draws attention to us rather than the greater good of humanity and Christ's kingdom. Archbishop Fulton Sheen once said that hospitals are filled with wasted suffering, and I would add that many homes are, too.[5] If your suffering is all about you, then nothing beyond you is accomplished; lives aren't changed.

Instead take a look at St. Paul's perspective. He knew his sufferings were for others' benefit, and that enabled him to rejoice through his pain (see Colossians 1:24). He knew he was filling up that which was lacking in the sufferings of Christ. St. James picks up on the same theme when he says, "Count it all joy, my brethren, when you meet various trials, for you know that the testing of your faith produces steadfastness. And let steadfastness have its full effect, that you may be perfect and complete, lacking in nothing" (James 1:2–4).

Remember that when you suffer you have the opportunity to be perfected. Once again, this is opposite of the way the world approaches pain. The world says pain is a setback—a hurdle that keeps you from becoming all you can be. But in the kingdom of God, suffering is a catalyst to be and do all you were meant to.

Perhaps you have tried "offering it up" many times in the past, but you never felt like anything happened. Because you didn't feel any different, you kind of gave up on the concept of joining your suffering with Christ. I know what you have experienced—I have been there. I found that what really made a difference for me was understanding what St. Paul said: "We walk by faith, not by sight" (2 Corinthians 5:7). The value of human suffering when it is joined to Christ is a mystery, and a mystery is something that is appropriated by faith.

Walking as Christ Walked

As Christians we do not allow circumstances or feelings to ultimately dictate or lead us. There are times we simply walk by faith by placing our trust in the principles of God's kingdom. This faith walk goes from the natural dimension to the supernatural dimension. The consolation we receive is the knowledge that something marvelous is happening in our lives, even if we don't feel anything or see the results we had hoped for. This is Christian maturity; this is walking as Christ walked.

Suffering gives you the opportunity to grow. Your trials give you a gift: the opportunity to become the person you always wanted to become. A holier person. A more patient person. A person who endures. A person who is kinder. A person who is more merciful. All of this is the fruit of suffering in your life.

A person who has suffered greatly and has appropriately faced his or her less-than-ideal situation becomes docile in the hands of God and very gentle and kind to others.

The word *passion* is used to describe multiple things. When talking about the final hours of Jesus earthly life, *passion* expresses the events that occurred as he poured out his life on the cross. Passion is also used to describe the love between and husband and wife. Passion is associated with suffering in both Jesus's love on the cross and the love between spouses.

When a married couple are passionate, about each other they are willing to suffer for each other as a demonstration of their great commitment. Fulton Sheen once said that there are three rings in marriage: the husband's ring, the wife's ring and "suffer-ring."[6] This is truer than we care to admit. Marriage is often the opportunity for a man and a woman to help each other grow in charity and character. If both husband and wife understand redemptive suffering, they can encourage each other to remain faithful and remind each other to offer up their suffering.

Practice Makes Perfect
The common phrase "practice makes perfect" is very apropos when it comes to suffering. Practice is key when trying to perfect any discipline in life, but in the area suffering, it might prove to be a lifesaving discipline.

When I was in high school, I struggled with math tests on a regular basis. My father, who has a Ph.D. in electrical engineering, was a math genius and actually found mathematics fun. We did not share a common fascination here—I couldn't find anything about it fun. For me it was in the category of suffering...intense suffering. I remember one thing my dad told me in the midst of my mathematical struggles. "Jeff," he said,

"If you study, practice, and really understand the material, you will not fear or dread tests; you will actually look forward to them." He could have been speaking Latin to me at that point, because I had such a negative attitude about math, but he was right.

One of the reasons we do not do well with suffering is that we face our problems once they become big problems, such as a health issue or a relationship issue. We tend to put up with low-grade suffering and don't address it—or I should say, "practice it?"

Many people would say the ultimate suffering is death. The fear of this ultimate suffering can immobilize us. As eternal beings, the thought of dying shakes us to the core, but with the certitude of eternal life in Christ, we can face death courageously. Even so, death is not a part of who we were created to be, so it will always be seen as a foreign experience. Fulton Sheen put it this way: "If death were merely a physical must, we would not fear it; our fear comes from the moral fact that we know we ought not to die. We fear death because it was not part of the original plan laid down for us."[7]

Perhaps Bishop Fulton Sheen gave the greatest piece of advice I have ever heard regarding how to deal with suffering. He said, "Death can be robbed of its greatest fearfulness if we practice for it. Christianity recommends mortification, penance, and detachment as a rehearsal for the great event.... The basic spiritual principle is this, that death must be conquered in every thought and word and deed by an affirmation of the eternal."[8]

In the same way, the greatest way to prepare for "serious" suffering is to practice it on a daily basis. If you practice "offering it up" on a daily basis with your less-than-ideal days, you will be better prepared to face and successfully navigate through your more intense suffering moments. Essentially the daily life of a Christian should be composed of multiple opportunities to practicing suffering. Putting this into biblical language, "The daily life of a Christian should really be composed of opportunities to pick up one's cross and follow Christ." At first you may think this is a weak and unpleasant way to live, but as author Arthur McGill states:

> The distinctive mark of God's power is service and self-giving. And in this world such power belongs only to him who serves. In the light of such a faith, the Christian has no final fear before the pretentious claims of violent power.[9]

The story of Zach Sobiech has had a profound impact on my life, as it has on millions of others. Zach, a young teenage boy from Stillwater, Minnesota, found out at age fourteen that he had osteosarcoma, a bone cancer that mostly strikes children. Zach demonstrated faith, hope, and charity in his nearly four-year battle with cancer. On May 20, 2013, Zach won his final battle and went on to be with the Lord. His hope of heaven was eloquently put to music in his number one hit, "Clouds." The song went to number one on iTunes, and at the time of Zach's death had over 3 million views on YouTube. Laura Sobiech, Zach's mother wrote about the struggle of suffering when one of your children is suffering. She said, "While I had chosen to trust God, to hope rather than despair, fear still reared up inside me. The practical part of trusting God is hard and takes practice."[10] Both Zach and his family got a lot of practice in trusting God. What God did in and through this young man will have profound eternal consequences in the lives of many.

Don't Suffer Alone

One of the keys to suffering well is to resist the temptation to isolate yourself and build walls around your heart. Proverbs 18:19 says, "A brother helped is like a strong city, but quarreling is like the bars of a castle." In John 15:5 Jesus states very clearly: "Apart from me you can do nothing."

In the midst of your suffering, ask yourself these questions:

Do I feel like I must go through this alone?

Do I isolate myself?

Do I reject help?

Does the bitterness in my heart cause me to push away those who come to me with beautiful words of comfort?

Do my discomfort and pain make me feel that no one could possibly understand what I'm going through?

Remember, without Jesus you can't do it. But with him you can do all things. Paul knew this secret to living in good times and in difficult times: "I can do all things in him who strengthens me" (Philippians 4:13).

The nightly news too often reports stories of people who feel isolated and discouraged to the point of taking their own lives—and sometimes the lives of their loved ones. Suffering in isolation leads to despair; suffering in union with Christ leads to strength and hope.

During a period when I was discouraged and felt depressed about certain issues in my life, I went to a professional Minnesota hockey game. There I was, sitting in the midst of eighteen thousand people, with everyone around me yelling and screaming and enjoying the game. Everyone seemed so alive, and yet I, with my suffering, felt so isolated and alone in the midst of that crowd. Many people feel isolated even though they are in a crowd. And a lot of that has to do with the fact that they have built a barrier around themselves. They don't allow people to encourage them. They don't allow people to guide them and direct them to the Lord, and in the end they actually become even more bitter and full of pain.

There's nothing intrinsically virtuous about being sick or in pain—it's what we choose to do with our pain that counts. Being honest when we're suffering is vital; this helps us avoid isolating ourselves. We can acknowledge the fact that what we're going through is painful and difficult, but we can also be courageous and turn to Christ. We can choose to not squander this opportunity but instead embrace it.

Journaling can be an effective way to express what we are feeling and what the Lord is doing in our heart. Remember, the purpose of suffering and the strategy in suffering is not just to get through it; it's to grow in Christ. It's to become holier, to become more perfect as Christ is perfect.

So the real goal in suffering—beyond wanting it to end—is becoming aware of what God is accomplishing in your life through it. It's asking, "Lord, what are you doing in me now? Are you converting a part of my life? Are you drawing me interiorly close to you? Is this about intimacy with you? Is this about becoming holier?"

That's what John Paul II said would happen. Brother Lawrence, a lowly monk in a Carmelite abbey, once said, "The greater perfection a soul aspires after, the more dependent on divine grace."[11] It's God's grace and his power in the midst of our suffering that perfects our souls.

Behold, Your Mother!

Anytime we go through suffering, we're faced with a decision. Do you wall yourself off from grace, or do you make a decision to go where Christ is? One of the wisest decisions you can make is to turn to his Mother.

Mary endured an incredible amount of suffering. What is interesting about her suffering is that it was predicted when Jesus was still a baby. When Mary and Joseph presented Jesus in the temple, a righteous and devout priest named Simeon was filled with the Spirit and spoke some sobering words to Mary.

> Simeon blessed them and said to Mary his mother,
> "Behold, this child is set for the fall and rising of many
>   in Israel,
> and for a sign that is spoken against
> (and a sword will pierce through your own soul also),
> that the thoughts out of many hearts may be revealed."
> (Luke 2:34–35)

Think about it: Mary, the mother of God, the woman with no sin, was told that she would suffer greatly. If Mary, who knew no sin and is considered the masterpiece of God, is to suffer, then we who have sinned can look to her as the perfect human model of what to do with our suffering. The Blessed Virgin Mary stayed with Jesus; she did not suffer alone. We find her at the foot of the cross, suffering with her Son, the second person of the Trinity.

This has distinct echoes from Genesis 3:15 where God says to the serpent, "I will put enmity between you and the woman, and between your seed and her seed; he shall bruise your head, and you shall bruise his heel." Way back in Genesis, we see that the very solution to sin involves suffering. Mary is the seed of the woman, working with her Son to redeem the world. Mary's love is also a perfect reflection of the love of God in a human being. She suffered with Jesus for us. But there was something different about Mary's suffering: As was true of the sacrifice of her Son, all her suffering was for others. She didn't need to offer up any suffering for herself. She didn't need to be perfected; she didn't need to be set free from sin. Therefore, her suffering was all for others, and she willingly said, "Lord, be it done onto me according to your will."

This was Mary's fiat, her "yes." If you compare yourself to Our Lady, you'll begin to notice everything in your life that needs to be eliminated so the image of God can clearly be seen. Like Michelangelo working on a sculpture, what needs to be removed from the block of the marble in order for a beautiful figure to emerge? What needs to go away? Everything that is not fiat needs to be subtracted. With our fiat, we give our yes to God; we give him permission to remove anything from our life that hinders his will. Mary is the perfect model of pure fiat and fruitful suffering.

At the foot of the cross, Mary demonstrated love for others, second only to that of Jesus himself. She participated with him and, by an act of her will, suffered. It was at that place of suffering, the cross, that Jesus announced to Mary, "Woman, behold, your son" and to his beloved disciple John, "Behold, your mother!" (see John 19:26–27). As Jesus offers the ultimate sacrifice, he shares his mother with the Church. If Jesus gave her to us at the greatest place of pain, no matter how much pain you might be in, you can go with confidence to Mary, knowing she understands. If she was able to stand at the foot of Jesus's cross, is she able to stand at the foot of yours?

It's because Mary is the queen of martyrs that we beg her to pray for us now and at the hour of our death each time we pray the Hail Mary. It was at the hour of her Son's death that she stood in the gap and suffered; with every rosary we pray, we're praying for that hour in our own life, and she's a part of it. This is a beautiful and very powerful truth. In the midst of suffering, the rosary becomes a powerful tool.

One of the three crosses on Calvary was wasted because the second thief, instead of imitating his companion by prayerful acceptance of his trial, rebelled against God and blasphemed him (see Luke 23:39). The good thief demonstrated one of the immediate effects of prayer in time of trial: the ability to spontaneously offer God whatever is so difficult to bear. We see the good thief uniting his suffering with the suffering of Christ.

The Role of the Holy Spirit

The Holy Spirit plays a significant role in our lives when we suffer. The Holy Spirit is always at work to replicate Christ's life within each one of us. He is continually pouring out the love of God into our hearts. Why? So we become like Christ. As St. John Paul II says about the Holy Spirit's relationship to suffering, "Suffering cannot be transformed and changed by a grace from outside, but from within. And Christ through his own salvific suffering is very much present in every human suffering and can act from within that suffering by the powers of his spirit of truth, his consoling spirit."[12]

The Holy Spirit is continually working in your life to conform you to the life, death, resurrection, and eternal glory of the Lord Jesus Christ. Said another way, the Holy Spirit is reproducing the life, death, resurrection, and eternal glory in your life. Jesus's life is your life, his suffering is your suffering, his resurrection is your resurrection, and his eternal glory is yours now. Once you understand the work of the Holy Spirit in your life, you will respond with a humble and willing spirit by offering up your suffering. A simple prayer in the midst of suffering, such as "Holy Spirit, conform me to the sufferings of Christ" can prove very helpful in your quest for holiness. You will think differently and suffer differently knowing that the Holy Spirit is accomplishing great things through you. This awareness of the work of the Holy Spirit is not a one-time occurrence, but a truth that needs to be acknowledged and renewed daily.

Also remember that the Holy Spirit is a consoling spirit. He is present to console you in your suffering, and at the same time, he is busy transforming you—not from the outside, but from within. He is making you like Christ. Typically when people suffer in our culture today, they look outside themselves for the answer. What outward source can change the way I'm feeling? What outside remedies can I find? The answer all along has been an inside job. It's the Holy Spirit working in your life, drawing you close to Christ, transforming you, and consoling you. Walking in the power of the Holy Spirit is key in the midst of your suffering.

While suffering will always be part of life on earth to one degree or another, it doesn't have to destroy you. Instead, recognizing that you are called to share in the sufferings of Christ can transform any situation into a grace-filled experience of God's love. With Mary at your side and the Holy Spirit at work within you, you can be "more than conquerors through him who loved us" (Romans 8:37).

Chapter Eight

WHEN YOU SUFFER

Prayer is essential at all times, but especially when you suffer. By prayerfully offering to God what is difficult, you are able to consciously unite your will with the will of God. What transforms suffering and makes it endurable—and even sweet—is intimacy with the Lord. St. Peter explains how we can entrust ourselves to Christ in the midst of suffering:

> To this you have been called, because Christ also suffered for you, leaving you an example, that you should follow in his steps. He committed no sin; no guile was found on his lips. When he was reviled, he did not revile in return; when he suffered, he did not threaten; but he trusted to him who judges justly. (1 Peter 2:21–23)

When Jesus suffered, he trusted himself to his Father. Peter, following Jesus's pattern, said, "Therefore let those who suffer according to God's will do right and entrust their souls to a faithful Creator" (1 Peter 4:19). What could be clearer than this? This is the prescription given to us by St. Peter for when we suffer—this is the true remedy.

It's interesting that Peter uses the word *Creator* in the above verse—this ties it back to Adam and Eve's fall, the result of which was that they lost trust in their Creator. Not being able to trust God during a time of suffering adds to the agony; suffering without God is a very lonely place.

Without trust in your heavenly Father, you cannot attach meaning to your suffering and can easily enter into despair. But with trust there is cause for rejoicing, even in the midst of trials. "Rejoice in so far as you share Christ's suffering, that you may also rejoice and be glad when his glory is revealed" (1 Peter 4:13).

Prayer and Perseverance

In order to experience the rejoicing, however, we must develop perseverance. The tendency to focus on ourselves is magnified during times of illness, pain, or stress. There's no getting around it: suffering tests our faith. It's important to remember what St. Paul said: "We rejoice in our sufferings, knowing that suffering produces endurance, and endurance produces character, and character produces hope, and hope does not disappoint us, because God's love has been poured into our hearts through the Holy Spirit who has been given to us" (Romans 5:3–5).

Suffering does not automatically draw us closer to God. In fact, suffering often results in us turning away from God and concentrating wholly on ourselves. It is enduring in the midst of suffering that develops character. Peter Kreeft says the worst thing about sickness is not physical pain in the body, but the narrowing of interest in the soul.[1] It is as if pain is a tyrant with a whip, crying, "Look at me, look at me!" every moment. And in those moments, you can either turn to yourself or you can turn to God. The situation can become all about you, which is going to result in nothing fruitful. Or it can turn your attention to God, resulting in an abundance of fruit. Instead of your inner dialogue being a continual "Look at me, look at me," change your perspective and begin to "look at him, look at him." You can choose to tell Jesus, "I join you; I willingly join you," instead of pitying yourself in the hopes that others will pity you, too. Resist that kind of introspection and begin meditating in a positive, holy way on Christ.

What is the worst thing that has ever happened in the world? Deicide—the crucifixion of God. That shocking event over two thousand years ago ended up becoming the greatest event in the history of the world. It resulted in the salvation of the world. If the greatest evil can work for the greatest good, then your sufferings can work for good in your life. "We know that in everything God works for good with those who love him" (Romans 8:28).

Polished to Perfection

One of the goals of suffering is perfection. God wants us to be perfect as he is perfect (see Matthew 5:48). The way to perfection is to become like Christ, and that involves enduring the cross; there is no perfection outside of the cross. None.

The goal of perfection is not an option meant only for super saints. The prerequisite for heaven is perfection, because nothing impure can enter heaven. God will not compromise with your life; he will have his way with you. The only other alternative is hell. Suffering focuses us on God and brings our wills into union with his. What isn't purified here on earth will be taken care of in purgatory. The choice is ours. Will we become saints the short way or the long way?

Jesus in the Garden of Gethsemane demonstrated something very powerful. He was one person with two natures: human and divine. The council of Constantinople also determined that Jesus had two wills: a human will and a divine will. But never at any point were these two at odds with each other. Jesus's human will was in constant harmony with the will of his Father (the divine will). In the Garden of Gethsemane, Jesus essentially said, "Father, if there's another way, let's do it. Nevertheless, your will be done."

Suffering well means that we marshal our will and bring our will into union with God's will. Our own suffering takes on the flavor of Gethsemane, and there we naturally look for an out. But we must come to the same conclusion Jesus did. "Nevertheless, your will be done. I entrust myself to you, Jesus. I trust you, Jesus. Jesus, I trust in you." St. John Paul II, who was acquainted with so much suffering, was also the pope who brought the Divine Mercy message to the forefront along with the work of St. Faustina. I believe this was because he was acquainted with suffering himself and needed to bring that message of trust to with the rest of the world.

Remember that what Christ accomplished on the cross—the greatest, most generous, most heroic achievement, the one that touches the life of every human being alive or dead—appeared to those who witnessed it to be a complete defeat. Pope Pius XII reminded those who were "afflicted with the burden of appearing to be useless" that this attitude is only outwardly true. How many senior citizens today feel useless, a burden to those around them? After retirement, many feel that the race is over, not realizing that they are still in the game! Now that the focus is no longer on work, retirees are so much more available to their children and grandchildren, their parish and community. They have so much more time for prayer and in some cases they live with regret about how they raised their own children. Offering up suffering for children and grandchildren can be a wonderful way to continue to love.

The Trinity Is a Family

Something else that brings meaning to our suffering is the understanding that the Trinity is not a solitude; it's a family. Father, Son, and Holy Spirit joyfully joined in a union of love. The Father loves the Son, and the Son responds in love to the Father. The very love between the Father and the Son is the Holy Spirit. What is beautiful is that Christ allows us to participate in his cross through our suffering because that is the way he allows us to participate in the exchanges of the Trinity. In the love of the Trinity we participate in that dynamo of love by offering up our own crosses. We share in the very inner life of God when we participate with our suffering.

Once you understand the power and the beauty of the cross—that it provides you with an opportunity to love as God loves—you will want to embrace that cross willingly and lovingly. Ask yourself today if would you be willing to carry Christ's cross, knowing it's an opportunity to love as Christ loves? Knowing it's an opportunity to share in the inner life of the Trinity, how does this change the way you view difficult situations or less than ideal days in your life?

After I had surgery on my neck, Good Friday took on a whole new meaning. I felt that I finally understood the meaning of suffering. When I went up to venerate the cross, as I placed my hand on the wood, it was such a powerful experience for me that I started to weep. And then, for the first time, I kissed the cross—really kissed it. It was not just some kind of pious devotion that I was told to do; it was an act of love and participation. Kissing the cross was my yes; it was saying, "Jesus, I will love the way you love. I will be with you in redeeming the world. I want to carry your cross."

The world doesn't understand this—they don't "get" us. But Jesus said, "If any man would come after me, let him deny himself and take up his cross daily and follow me" (Luke 9:23). This is not some silver or twenty-four-karat gold cross—that's an easy cross. Jesus told us, "In the world you have tribulation; but be of good cheer, I have overcome the world" (John 16:33). He overcame the world through the cross, and as a result, our existence on earth is lived with the hope of eternal life.

Hope in Suffering

Along with understanding suffering, having hope in the midst of suffering is the key to suffering well. Because humans are limited in their knowledge of the future and aware of the possibility of multiple scenarios for their future, they are hopeful, for they naturally seek fulfillment and meaning in life. We are made to hope. God has placed hope within us.

Professional sports illustrates that we are hopeful beings. The greatest quarterbacks complete only six out of ten passes. The best basketball players only make about 50 percent of their shots. Major league baseball players make first base only 40 percent of the time, and that includes walks. Why do they continue pursuing their sport with so many failures? Hope!

Becoming discouraged is very common, but you must resist discouragement and despair. Despair and presumption are contrary to hope; the *Catechism of the Catholic Church* tells us that despair and presumption are sins against hope (CCC 2091). The reason that despair is a sin against hope is because despair is contrary to God's goodness and justice, for the Lord is faithful to his promises.

There are two kinds of presumption that will thwart the value of redemptive suffering. First, when a person presumes upon his own capacities by placing his hope in his own ability to save himself without God's help, in effect this places God out of the picture. Secondly, when a person hopes in God without conversion of heart, he or she essentially presumes the help of God without doing one's part. As this pertains to suffering, if a person hopes for something good to result from suffering without actively participating with God by offering it up, it is a presumptive act.

To hope in God goes beyond the common understanding of hope today. If someone were to ask you if tomorrow is going to be a good day, you might respond, "I hope so." This kind of hope is more like wishful thinking. The hope that Christians exercise is a hope that is not uncertain but certain, because the point of reference is the finished work of Christ. Connected to hope is a deep trust that God is working in you for the greater good. If your point of reference for the future were only the result of your experience and skill set, it would be presumption.

The Bible gives us a number of ways that people misplace their hope. Some people put their hope in riches (see 1 Timothy 6:17). Some put their hope in men (see Psalm 118:8). Some put their hope in idols (see Jeremiah 48:13). And some put their hope in created things (see Ps 33:17). There is a big problem with putting your hope in these things: You will be disappointed, and your heart will be let down. Proverbs 13:12 says, "Hope deferred makes the heart sick, but a desire fulfilled is a tree of life."

You might find yourself thinking in the midst of your suffering, "I'm hopeless." I've got news for you—if you have been baptized, you are not hopeless. At baptism you received three major ingredients to help you in your suffering. The Church calls these ingredients *theological virtues*. They are faith, hope, and charity. All three can be used to help you offer up your suffering.

> The Most Holy Trinity gives the baptized sanctifying grace, the grace of *justification*:
> —enabling them to believe in God, to hope in him, and to love him through the theological virtues;
> —giving them the power to live and act under the prompting of the Holy Spirit through the gifts of the Holy Spirit;
> —allowing them to grow in goodness through the moral virtues.
> Thus the whole organism of the Christian's supernatural life has its roots in Baptism (CCC 1266).

Faith is exercised when you place your trust in God in the midst of your ordeal. Charity is extended to others by offering up your suffering. Hope is expressed by the expectation that God will give you the capacity to be divinely blessed in the midst of your suffering and ultimately receive the beatific vision of God—that is, being with him in heaven forever. When you are tempted to give up, think about these two truths: (1) there is divine blessing in your suffering, and (2) you have the beatific vision to look forward to.

St. Paul told the Colossians that hope was stored up for them in heaven (see Colossians 1:4–5). To the Romans he wrote: "May the God of hope fill you with all joy and peace in believing, so that by the power of the Holy Spirit you may abound in hope" (Romans 15:13).

Often people feel out of control during times of suffering. Frankly, this is one of the big challenges of suffering. You can see your life as out of control, or you can willingly give up control and give it to Christ. This is a good time to remind yourself of what the writer of Hebrews said: "We have this as a sure and steadfast anchor of the soul, a hope that enters into the inner shrine behind the curtain" (Hebrews 6:19). Hope is an anchor that keeps you stable, and it gives you the assurance that you will not drift. The winds can howl and the rain can pour, but you will stay put because you are anchored. Remind yourself in the midst of trials that you have the anchor of hope to keep you stable.

Zach Sobiech's mother understood the power of hope as a stabilizing force in the worst storm of her life:

> I wanted my children to see how a life lived in faith could bring hope to the world around them, that acting out of love rather than fear would allow Christ to shine through them without ever having to say a word. And to know that joy—not just happiness, but true joy— comes when we give up our own agenda and let God work through us. Then we can begin to see the bigger

picture, the eternal picture, rather than just the tiny brush stroke of our own lives.[2]

Hope is related to trust and the willingness to let go and let God. Zach's story is "about a boy who learned to live while dying and in doing so brought hope to countless people who desperately needed it."[3]

> Okay, Lord. You can have Zach. I want him, but you see a bigger picture. If Zach must die, please just let it be for something big. I want it to be for something big. Just one soul changed forever." At that moment, my soul was freed. I wasn't in charge of this thing, and in the depths of my being, I truly understood the meaning of hope.[4]

> Hope is something much bigger than anything physical we may desire. It is about raising our eyes from a point on the horizon to the heavens and into eternity. And it's about relying on God's grace to do it, no matter what the cost.[5]

A Scripture I often meditate on in the midst of my own less-than-ideal days is Jeremiah 29:11: "For I know the plans I have for you, says the Lord, plans for welfare and not for evil, to give you a future and a hope."

Suffering Engages You in Real Life

In my experience I have found that many men are perplexed about how they can offer their suffering up for others when they don't particularly know a lot of theology. Being a man of

God who is willing to love is not dependent upon degrees or a graduate level understanding of the Bible. In his bestselling book, *Wild at Heart*, John Eldredge argues that there are three things every man has a desire for:[6]

A Battle to Fight: Men want to fiercely struggle for worthy goals. At heart, boys and men are warriors who secretly aspire to William Wallace (*Braveheart*) status.

An Adventure to Live: Men love to go on adventures and take on the challenges that life presents. Epic films such as Indiana Jones or Moby Dick appeal to the desire for adventure in most of us.

A Beauty to Rescue: Women provide a source for inspiration. Most men want to show the woman in their life that they will protect and care for them.

Whether you agree with John Eldredge's three desires or not, I think that his assessment of men is useful in light of finding a context for suffering. As a man who has observed my wife's willingness to suffer hardships for our family, I am quite aware that she suffers better that I do. Knowing there are a lot of men just like me, allow me to target my comments here primarily to men.

The greatest battle in the world today is the battle for human souls. There really is an enemy, Satan, who prowls about desiring the ruin of souls. Jesus Christ is the Messiah who takes on more than a country like Egypt, Assyria, the Greeks, or Romans. Unlike his predecessors such as Judas Maccabeus, Jesus takes on sin and the enemy of all enemies, Satan. We see this demonstrated in Matthew 4 when Jesus goes out into the wilderness and is tempted by the devil. In all three temptations, Jesus answers with the Word of God and emerges triumphant. The great victory was won at the cross and resurrection! The great battle for the salvation of souls, invites men (and women) to enter the arena of real life and fight against evil. St. John Paul II said, "Salvation means liberation from evil, and for this reason it is closely bound up with the problem of suffering."[7] Evil was overcome by love, a love that was willing to suffer. If men would engage in this epic struggle of good versus evil, and if they would think of the eternal good for their families and friends, they may just find themselves in a battle worth fighting for...and living for.

One of the great hardships of childhood is being bored. Children surrounded by gadgets, toys, and candy still find themselves bored with nothing to do. I'm afraid that many adults also suffer from this paralyzing plight. Caught somewhere between the tyranny of the urgent and boredom, many men experience a lack of adventure in their lives. The common midlife crisis often propels men to find some kind of adventure that will fulfill this deep desire. While there are many adventures one could embark upon and many things that can be bought or experienced, the greatest adventure—following Christ and living his life—is the one that will never leave a person empty. The unfortunate thing is that all too often men engage in destructive adventures that ironically bring more suffering into their lives. I would dare to say that if Christ were here on earth with us, the same way he was with the disciples, we would not be so fascinated with cars at age fifty. Each and every day, Christ invites us to yield our lives to him and allow him to adventure out into the world through us. St. Paul put it this way: "I have been crucified with Christ; it is no longer I who live, but Christ who lives in me; and the life I now live in the flesh I live by faith in the Son of God, who loved me and gave himself for me" (Galatians 2:20).

Looking for a beauty to rescue? The first Adam failed to rescue his beauty, Eve. He stood by silently while the enemy dismantled their relationship with God, with each other, and creation. The second Adam, Jesus Christ, did not stand by and watch the destruction of his bride. Jesus died for his beauty, the Church. If you want to become more like Christ, learn to offer up the less-than-ideal situations in your life as a sacrifice for the Church. If you are married, see your wife as the beautiful God-given treasure she is. If you have daughters, see them as the beauties you are willing to sacrifice for. Many men might be willing to die for their ladies, but the real question is, are you willing to live for them? Dietrich Bonhoeffer once said, "We must form our estimate of men less from their achievements and failures, and more from their sufferings."[8]

Who Will Receive the Fruit of Your Suffering?

Identify those in your life that you care about and would like to offer your suffering for. Remember, St. John Paul II said, "The springs of divine power gush forth precisely in the midst of human weakness. Those who share in the sufferings of Christ preserved in their own sufferings a very special *particle of the infinite treasure* of the world's redemption, and can share this treasure with others."[9]

In your suffering, you have such a beautiful chance to walk as Our Lord walked and love as he loves. In the midst of your pain and suffering, you have the opportunity to really make a difference in the lives of others. Think of your suffering as a treasure that you can spend on them. You can simply turn on the news and see the suffering that is happening around the world. You can pick up the paper and identify people who need God's intervention in their lives. Whether it's Twitter, Facebook, or Instagram, we all hear about tragedies that need the Lord Jesus Christ. You could be that one who notices the pain in the world and responds with a gift that can change the world. Think about it…Jesus died for the world, and you now have the eyes and heart of Christ and can offer your pain, in union with his, to bring salvation to the world.

From your living room or from your car, you can connect to those who are going through unspeakable agony by saying, "Lord, take my pain and apply it to the person I saw on the news or the woman I read about in the paper." As I was writing this book, I heard about four young Christians in Iraq who would not deny Christ at the hands of ISIS terrorists. As a consequence of their decision to remain faithful to Christ, they were beheaded. I can't imagine the pain their parents went through. I offered my less-than-ideal day, my moral and physical suffering, up for them and their loved ones.

How often has a mother or father said, "I would gladly trade places with my son or daughter?" when their children are in pain. Speaking of trading places, think about Simon the Cyrene. The Bible says he was pressed into service to assist Jesus to carrying his cross (see Matthew 27:32). By carrying the cross he was serving Jesus. Wow! When you see a news story, hear about your relatives, read an email about a tragedy in a colleague's family—are you being pressed into service? Once you understand the power of the cross, you will embrace it. Now you can know that 100 percent of your life matters! You are significant on the world's stage! How many people today, if given the chance, would cooperate with Christ as Simon did? And just like Simon, to participate in the actual crucifixion of Christ for the salvation of all humankind is the opportunity before you.

Conceal and Carry

In the midst of your suffering, it is good to remain mindful of those around you and any circumstances where you could offer up your suffering for others.

I'm reminded of what St. Paul said to the Corinthians:

> Blessed be the God and Father of our Lord Jesus Christ, the Father of mercies and God of all comfort, who comforts us in all our affliction, so that we may be able to comfort those who are in any affliction, with the comfort with which we ourselves are comforted by God. For as we share abundantly in Christ's sufferings, so through Christ we share abundantly in comfort too. (2 Corinthians 1:3–5)

This truth came home to me when I was being prepped for emergency surgery on my neck. I was lying on my back in the prep room as the nurse inserted the IV into my arm. I couldn't move my neck at all, and I couldn't even lift my head due to the pain in my neck and arm. Because I couldn't look around, I was not aware that other patients were also being prepped for surgery. Then, next to me I heard the sound of a young woman crying quietly. By this time I had come to realize the power of redemptive suffering, and I had begun to walk with a new awareness of the opportunity to love as Christ loves by uniting my suffering with his. Hearing the young woman next to me weeping, I recognized the opportunity in that cold surgery prep room, and my feelings of trepidation turned to joy as I focused my attention on her.

Without knowing who she was or what she looked like or how far away she was from me, I reached out to her by saying, "Hello?" She said hello back to me, and as it turned out, she couldn't see at me either. I asked her if she was being prepared for surgery, and she said, "Yes." without thinking I asked, "For what?" I'm not suggesting that men should ask women about the nature of their surgery—I just blurted it out. Holding back tears and sniffling, she said, "I'm getting my neck fused, C6-7. Rather awkwardly but with sincere enthusiasm, I encouraged her with, "Me, too!"

I asked, "Are you scared?" With a sob, she said, "Yes." I asked if she believed in God, and she said that she did. I told her that I did, too, and that I was a Christian. I then asked if I could pray for her. She responded, "Please." Without being able to see each other, I proceeded, "In the name of the Father and the Son and the Holy Spirit," and then I began to pray for her surgery, the surgeon, and her outcome, and then I ended the prayer with, "In the name of the Father and the Son and the Holy Spirit, Amen." We both were taken off to separate operating rooms.

The day after my surgery, I found out the hard way that there are two ways of doing spinal fusions. One is to replace the old disc with the patient's own hipbone, shaped into a disc. The other is by taking a cadaver bone and replacing the damaged disc. By using a cadaver bone, the patient is relatively pain-free after surgery and walking normally within hours. On the other hand, using the patient's hipbone leaves the patient with pain in the hip—a lot of pain! When I woke up I thought I was pain-free until I tried to move my hip—suddenly I shrieked as I grabbed my hip and rang for a nurse. When the nurse came to my side, I told her that something was terribly wrong with my hip. I told her I thought there might be a needle stuck in my hip somehow. She informed me that the surgeon operated on my hip too. This led to two or three months of limping and quite a bit of pain.

The day after surgery I got out of bed, heading over to the bathroom for the first time. As many people know, a directionally challenged fashion designer designed most hospital gowns. Discreet was not the theme of this gown. But remember, all of this also can be considered suffering. As I carefully made my way to the bathroom, I suddenly heard the voice of the woman in the surgery prep room, the one I prayed for.

"Hello!" she said in a loud, enthusiastic voice. I quickly gathered my gown and slowly turned around. I wasn't completely sure it was that woman until she said, "I'm the one you prayed with." She was jumping around like a little gazelle. Obviously she was the recipient of a cadaver bone!

She had gratitude written all over her face as she expressed how thankful she was that I prayed with her prior to her surgery. She said, "It meant the world to me when you prayed." Offering up your suffering for others can be a very generous gift of love. Oftentimes people tell me they don't know how to share their faith with others. Perhaps they are shy, or they just don't feel they are theologically equipped to start a conversation. But suffering gives you an open door into the interior life of others. St. John Paul II put it this way:

> Down through the centuries and generations it has been seen that in suffering there is concealed a particular power that draws a person interiorly close to Christ, a special grace.... It is suffering, more than anything else, which clears the way for the grace which transforms human souls.[10]

If you are suffering and meet others who need the grace of God, remember that you are carrying a concealed weapon that can result in eternal life. If you are a Christian, you have been given a conceal-and-carry permit for sharing your faith through your suffering.

Chapter Nine

KEEPING IT REAL:
TEN THINGS TO DO WHEN YOU SUFFER

Much of this book has dealt with the biblical and theological aspects of suffering in order to provide a solid framework for understanding its place in your own life. Having such an understanding is key to developing an intimate relationship of union with Christ, as well as being able to process the suffering you encounter in your own life and in the lives of those around you. In this chapter we'll turn our attention to ten practical ways you can make suffering meaningful and transformative.

1. Entrust Yourself to God

One of the best things you can do when you are in the midst of a difficult situation is to go before the Blessed Sacrament in an Adoration Chapel. Many Catholic churches have a separate chapel set aside for prayer. On the altar is the Blessed Sacrament held in a monstrance. As Catholics, we believe that the Blessed Sacrament, consecrated during Mass, is the very body, blood, soul, and divinity of our Lord Jesus Christ. This means that in the Blessed Sacrament, Jesus is truly present with us. The beautiful thing about adoration is that it gives you a chance to physically sit in front of the Lord and entrust yourself to him. Just sit in quiet contemplation, meditating on Jesus and the work he did on the cross. By an act of your will, pray this simple prayer:

> Jesus, I'm choosing to entrust myself to you in the midst of this battle, this suffering. I refuse to blame others or run away or self-medicate or become bitter. Instead I will entrust myself to you, and I will allow you to work in me however you want. Please bring about the results you desire.

St. Peter tells us, "Therefore let those who suffer according to God's will do right and entrust their souls to a faithful Creator" (1 Peter 4:19). As an aid to help you entrust yourself to Jesus, especially during tough times, you can also pray the Divine Mercy Chaplet. On February 22, 1931, Jesus Christ appeared to this simple nun, Sister Faustina, and introduced her to a wonderful message of Mercy for all the world. St. Faustina tells of the moment in her diary:

> In the evening, when I was in my cell, I became aware of the Lord Jesus clothed in a white garment. One hand was raised in blessing, the other was touching the garment at the breast. From beneath the garment, there were emanating two large rays, one red, the other pale. In silence I kept my gaze fixed on the Lord; my soul was struck with awe, but also with great joy. After a while, Jesus said to me, "Paint an image according to the pattern you see, with the signature: Jesus, I trust in You."[1]

Sister Faustina was a young, uneducated nun in a convent of the Congregation of Sisters of Our Lady of Mercy in Krakow, Poland, during the 1930s. She recorded her experiences, which she compiled in notebooks. Today these notebooks are known as the *Diary of Saint Maria Faustina Kowalska*, and the words she recorded reveal God's loving message of Divine Mercy.

In the year 2000, St. John Paul II canonized Sr. Faustina, making her the first saint of the new millennium. The Divine Mercy Chaplet, which is typically prayed at 3:00 p.m., is a unique devotion—it combines Christ's passion on the cross, God's mercy, and the theme of trusting in Christ. The second Sunday in Easter is when the Church now celebrates Divine Mercy around the world.

Remember, entrusting yourself to God isn't just saying the words "I trust you"—it's an act of the will that then plays out afterward with a continual attitude of trust. You don't trust and then take it back. The Blessed Mother trusted God through the message of the angel, and once she said yes, there were many more yeses to come. Therefore, when you initially entrust yourself to Jesus, be prepared to reiterate that trust and act on it the next day, the next week, the next month, and so on. You will have plenty of opportunities to be tested when you find yourself in pain.

2. Unite Your Will with the Will of Christ through Prayer

As in all areas of our life, Jesus is the model. The point where Jesus exercised his will in prayer in the midst of suffering was in the garden of Gethsemane.

> Then Jesus went with them to a place called Gethsemane, and he said to his disciples, "Sit here, while I go over

there and pray." And taking with him Peter and the two sons of Zebedee, he began to be sorrowful and troubled. Then he said to them, "My soul is very sorrowful, even to death; remain here, and watch with me." And going a little farther he fell on his face and prayed, "My Father, if it be possible, let this chalice pass from me; nevertheless, not as I will, but as thou will." (Matthew 26:36–39)

It is at this point that you must focus and discipline your thoughts. As I said earlier, take your thoughts captive and unite yourself to Christ. Jesus prayed before key moments in his ministry (see CCC 2600). Following his example, make your first reaction an action: pray.

Once again, this requires an act of the will. You do this not by just thinking it, but by confessing. Praying is saying. Just like Jesus—he didn't just think thoughts in the Garden of Gethsemane. He talked to his Father, expressing exactly how he felt. His whole being was involved in this prayer, even to the point of sweating blood. In the midst of your Gethsemane, tell your Heavenly Father, "Nevertheless, not my will, but your will be done," and in this way unite your will with the will of Christ. Stop for a moment right now and practice saying it: "Jesus, I unite my suffering with yours for the greater good of your mission." This may sound strange coming out of your mouth, but you'll get used to it. That's your responsibility. It's not your spouse's responsibility; it's not your pastor's responsibility; it's not your prayer group's responsibility. Only you can unite your will to the will of Christ. You can follow your words by meditating on the Scriptures to really make it real.

Identify your Gethsemane. Go to a place where you can replicate the life of Christ in your life. If you wear a crucifix, the moment something happens, clutch the crucifix and let it become a reminder to go to that place where Jesus made the decision to unite his will with the Father's will. If you carry a rosary, the moment something happens, pull out your rosary and begin praying the sorrowful mysteries; let this remind you of the sufferings of Christ. If you have a prayer book, open it and enter into prayer. Enter into Christ's prayer in the Garden of Gethsemane and say, "Not as I will, but as you will."

3. Realize That Jesus Will Not Allow You to Go through Something You Can't Handle

Things are never hopeless. There's always a way to deal with your suffering, and you don't need to do it alone. The apostle Paul, in 2 Corinthians 12:7–10, pleaded with the Lord to take away what he called a thorn in the flesh. He entreated the Lord three times. Remove it, remove it, remove it—and the answer was, "My grace is sufficient for you, for my power is made perfect in weakness" (2 Corinthians 12:9). That wasn't the answer Paul wanted to hear, but it's the answer he *needed* to hear. This brings up a good point about suffering. The answers you hear from the Church, from Christ, and from the saints are not answers you necessarily *want* to hear, but they are answers you *need* to hear.

God's grace is sufficient for anything the enemy can throw at you. There is not one situation in the world you could bring to God and have his response be, "My grace is not sufficient for this situation." Trust me. Your situation will never surprise God, nor will it leave him puzzled as to what to do.

What in your mind is the worst form of suffering that you can think of? Take a moment and think about what you would do. It's not that hard. You've already thought about what you would do in a great situation. You know what you would do if you won the lottery. You probably know what car you would buy, what charities you'd give to, which debts you would pay off. You have it down because you've rehearsed it many times. Now, what if you were in the worst situation possible? How would you spend your "heavenly cash"? Who would benefit from your suffering? Just as you rehearsed many times in your mind your exact lottery winning dispersion, now rehearse what you would do with your suffering. For whom would you offer your suffering? Do you necessarily have to like them? Have they been kind or unkind to you? Is this an opportunity to overcome unforgivingness and reward generosity? This is your opportunity to love those who may not have loved you. How will you unite your will with the will of the Father? How would you rely on God's grace? Remember, practice makes perfect.

4. Go to Confession

The key to walking in victory in the midst of suffering is a strong relationship with Jesus Christ. Sin, which "always involves a refusal of God's fatherly love and of his loving gifts"[2] will always result in division and pain. When we sin we are not merely denying God—to "sin is also to live as if he did not exist, to eliminate him from one's daily life"[3]

St. John Paul II describes how serious sin is when it comes to walking in wholeness. "As a rupture with God, sin is an act of disobedience by a creature who rejects, at least implicitly, the very one from whom he came and who sustains him in life. It is therefore a suicidal act. Since by sinning man refuses to submit to God, his internal balance is also destroyed and it is precisely within himself that contradictions and conflicts arise."[4]

He describes the internal consequences of sin that can result in moral suffering. "As a personal act, sin has its first and most important consequences in the sinner himself: that is, in his relationship with God, who is the very foundation of human life; and also in his spirit, weakening his will and clouding his intellect."[5]

Sin affects the soul, which can lead to unnecessary suffering. Instead of the intellect guiding the will by the light of truth, the intellect, influenced by sin, is darkened, and the will acts impetuously without gathering all the necessary data to make sound decisions.

Because sin is familial, it affects not only your relationship with God, but also with the entire human family. While sin is committed personally, it is perpetuated in community, which makes sin easier to commit as each generation passes. There really are no secret sins—every sin has repercussions that can reach far and wide.

But just as sin affects the whole human family, so receiving forgiveness and offering up our suffering can affect the whole human family, but in a positive way.

You don't want to go through suffering, whether moral or physical, knowing you have sin in your life that has not been dealt with. Unconfessed sin gives a landing place for the enemy and weakens our ability to think sharply and act wisely. The writer of the Epistle to the Hebrews said,

During the liturgy, before we offer up our suffering in union with Christ, we confess our sins to the Lord when we say the Confiteor:

I confess to almighty God
and to you, my brothers and sisters,
that I have greatly sinned
in my thoughts and in my words,
in what I have done
and in what I have failed to do,
through my fault,
through my fault,
through my most grievous fault; therefore I ask blessed
Mary ever-Virgin, all the Angels and Saints,
and you, my brothers and sisters,
to pray for me to the Lord our God.[6]

It's important to differentiate between the two kinds of sin: venial and mortal.

Venial sin weakens charity; it manifests a disordered affection for created goods; it impedes the soul's progress in the exercise of the virtues and the practice of the moral good; it merits temporal punishment.... "Venial sin does not deprive the sinner of sanctifying grace, friendship with God, charity, and consequently eternal happiness." (CCC 1863)

Mortal sin...results in the loss of charity and the privation of sanctifying grace, that is, of the state of grace. If it is not redeemed by repentance and God's forgiveness, it causes exclusion from Christ's kingdom and the eternal death of hell, for our freedom has the power to make choices for ever, with no turning back. (CCC 1861)

The result of mortal sin is definitive suffering: to be without God for eternity. As we covered earlier in the book, Jesus came and suffered death so that we would not endure definitive suffering. When it comes to suffering, the confession of sin always contributes to healing. If you do not know how to make a good confession, go to your priest and tell him and he will walk you through the steps. Priests are pleased to work with those who want to walk in healing and wholeness. The United States bishops have wonderful guidelines on their website, www.usccb.org.

So lighten your load. Don't carry sin into your suffering.

5. Participate on the Altar during Mass

During the Preparation of the Gifts, focus your thoughts and heart on the act of giving God your whole life. Often we suffer throughout the week, but then, when we come to Mass, we don't do anything in terms of offering our pain and suffering to him. This is our time to truly unite our sufferings with Christ, but how often do we miss this supernatural opportunity because of our many preoccupations? In the words of Fr. Rich Simon, "We act like we are sitting on a couch, rather than in a pew."[7] Sadly, we often attend Mass and leave carrying the very pain and suffering that we began with. In a sense, we act as though God were not interested in changing our pain into gain.

Mass is the place where great change can take place. This great change equals a great exchange. We bring bread and wine, and God gives us his body and blood. We give him our victories and suffering, and he gives us redemptive power to apply to friends and loved ones. At the time of the preparation of the gifts, when the bread and wine are slightly raised during the prayer, "Blessed are you, Lord God of all creation..." the host is left on the paten as a sign that it is offered to God so it may become the body and blood of Christ. This is the moment at Mass when you want to consciously offer your suffering to God and ask him to redeem it and make it salvific. This is done by an act of your will—it is a deliberate move to give God your victories as well as your sufferings by joining him on the paten. At the moment the patent is lifted up, you can take your suffering and offer it to God as a sacrifice. As the paten is elevated, so are your sufferings in offering to God. God can change your suffering into redemptive power, and you can join him in his mission to save the world (also see CCC 1350).

It's a good habit to prepare your heart on the way to Mass by taking note of the suffering, both moral and physical, that you have gone through during the week, consciously embracing it as the liturgy begins. Turn off all electronics and meditate on what you can offer God. By doing this you will have something of value to offer God, something he can use to change the world. Your thoughts will change from "Woe is me" to those of St. Paul: "I rejoice in my sufferings for your sake" (Colossians 1:24).

By the way, if you are a parent, this is an excellent time to talk to your children about their suffering and what it means in the context of the Holy Sacrifice of the Mass. In this age of entitlement, it is critical that parents teach their children about suffering and what to do with it. If they don't learn the value of suffering from their parents, they will find other ways of dealing with their pain as adults.

6. Take a Vocation, Not a Vacation!
Actively love by fulfilling and continuing to live according to your current vocation. As the *Catechism* says, "God who

created man out of love also calls him to love—the fundamental and innate vocation of every human being. For man is created in the image and likeness of God who is himself love" (CCC 1604).

God not only created humans out of love, he calls all of humankind to live this vocation of love. Keep in mind that we are called to love through our personal calling in life. The decision to serve God on earth through marriage, religious life, or a generous single life is a matter of discernment. Once the decision is made to get married or become a priest or religious, your state of life is called your vocation. The key to remember is that this universal vocation to love is expressed through one's personal vocation. For me, I'm called to love my wife and children because of my vocation as husband and father. As a husband and father, life will present me with unique opportunities to participate in and express the love of God.

Perhaps one of the most important things to remember in this book is the fact that just because you are suffering (whether morally or physically) does not give you an excuse to take a vacation from your vocation. If you are a wife, then that is what you are regardless of the intensity of your suffering.

Suffering is even more beautifully expressed when it is expressed through your vocation. Back in the 1960s the United States was embroiled in the civil rights movement. African Americans did not enjoy the same rights as white people. The message became very clear to the public when they actually saw African Americans being arrested, suffering for the freedom to which they were called.

On December 1, 1955, Rosa Parks, a forty-two-year-old African American in Montgomery, Alabama, boarded a city bus to go home. Because she refused to give up her seat on the basis of race, America more clearly understood the quest for freedom for the African American community because they witnessed a woman suffering for what is good and right. From that day on, citizens of Alabama were daily reminded of Rosa Parks every time they saw a city bus. Her decision that day was not planned; it was a spontaneous response to what she knew she was called to and what was right.

The key to the unlawful laws of segregation being overturned was not arguing or blaming, but simply allowing the public to witness the injustice. Many people were willing to suffer for what was right and true. When the public saw this display of courage, the popular opinion changed; the world changed. The willingness to remain faithful according to your vocation has world-changing consequences.

You see, suffering doesn't determine whether you're a mother, a wife, or a nun. But what you do with your suffering as a mother or wife or nun amplifies and clarifies the true nature of a mother, wife, and nun. If someone were to ask you to explain what it means to be a parent, you would never be as clear or convincing as you would if you could simply show them. By remaining true to your vocation in the midst of suffering, you send a clear message to those around you that you really are reflecting the love of God to the world.

Traditionally men have been very good at offering up their lives for their families when confronted with tragic circumstances. On the Titanic the number of men who survived was extremely low compared to the number of women and children. The statistics show that men sacrificed themselves for their families. There were 434 women on the Titanic, and 324 survived. There were 112 children, and 56 survived. There were 1,680 male passengers aboard the Titanic (taking into consideration that the majority of crew were male), and only 323 survived.[8] This means that 75 percent of the women on the Titanic survived, 50 percent of the children survived, and only 19 percent of the men survived. The statistics tell us that the men put their families first. Maybe men today should pretend their homes are the Titanic!

My Titanic moment took place the night I almost gave in to despair. I experienced severe neck issues when my three daughters were still living at home—one in high school and the other two in preschool. After having surgery, I came home knowing I would have to take it easy for a while.

That first night I went to bed after taking the drugs that the doctor gave me for the pain. I went to sleep on my side, a little fearful of what I'd feel like in the morning after the medication wore off. I couldn't help wondering what kind of excruciating pain I might face. At about five o'clock in the morning, something very uncharacteristic happened. My middle daughter, Jaki, came into our bedroom and made her way over to my side of the bed. Keep in mind that ninety-nine times out of a hundred, she went to my wife's side of the bed. This time she came to my side. Of all times to wake me up, why this one?

I think that parents have a radar system built in that alerts them when their children are within three inches of their faces while sleeping. Laying on my side, radar working, I opened my eyes, and there was Jaki staring at me, like a princess waiting for her servant to respond. I just groaned, but somehow my wife remained asleep. A bit foggy from the pain meds, I said, "Jaki, what do you want?"

She held up a naked Barbie doll and a pink dress. With a determination in her voice, Jaki said, "Just dress her and you can go back to sleep." I had a number of thoughts in my mind at that point. One of them was, "Please just go bother your mother."

This daughter never got up at 5:00 A.M. For some reason, though, she got up that morning and started playing with her dolls. The only problem was that she couldn't dress the Barbie doll by herself, and after thinking of who could possibly help her, I was the one she landed on. I kind of chuckled to myself and thought, *She thinks I'm her father. She actually thinks I'm going to function as her daddy right now. She has no idea what I just went through in the last forty-eight hours.* None of this was on her mind when she asked me to dress this precious toy of hers so early in the morning.

As I looked at her blurry but beautiful face, suddenly it became clear to me that this was an opportunity to love. My vocation to fatherhood meant nothing to her theologically, but it meant everything to her in terms of solving her problem. *I have a choice,* I thought. *Do I remain father, or do I tell her "Because I'm having difficulty I won't be your father this morning"?*

So I said, "Give her to me." I had no idea how to dress a Barbie doll, but somehow I managed to get the dress on. Then I said, "Now go back to your room, sweetie, and let me sleep, OK?" She said OK, and I closed my eyes, pleased with my heroic valor and finesse.

A minute or two later, the radar alerted me that she was back. "Daddy?" I opened my eyes, and she looked at me with a disappointing glare. "It's on backwards," she said.

I started laughing, and I ripped that dress off and put it on the right way. "Now, please let Daddy sleep," I said.

That early morning experience with Jaki was a lesson to me on how to love in and through my vocation as a father. I was able to love my daughter even though I was in pain and inconvenienced. Certainly that particular early morning was not an ideal time for me, but Jaki's need was real, and because I was able to help her, it was an ideal morning for her. Jaki didn't ponder my pain number before waking me up—she was just a little girl whose daddy could do anything.

I'm reminded of St. Paul:

> Are they servants of Christ? I am a better one — I am talking like a madman — with far greater labors, far more imprisonments, with countless beatings, and often near death. Five times I have received at the hands of the Jews the forty lashes less one. Three times I have been beaten with rods; once I was stoned. Three times I have been shipwrecked; a night and a day I have been adrift at sea; on frequent journeys, in danger from rivers, danger from robbers, danger from my own people, danger from Gentiles, danger in the city, danger in the wilderness, danger at sea, danger from false brethren; in toil and hardship, through many a sleepless night, in hunger and thirst, often without food, in cold and exposure. And, apart from other things, there is the daily pressure upon me of my anxiety for all the churches. (2 Corinthians 11:23–28)

See? I'm right up there with St. Paul now! Once I changed a Barbie doll in the early morning hours while in great pain.

7. Pray the Rosary

Have you ever noticed how people like to share their war stories with each other? I've sat in groups before where one person tells the group about his breaking his leg back when he was in college. The next person then brings up her car accident, only to be followed by her friend who had his legs, arms, and head amputated in a farming accident. Luckily all limbs and head were reattached in time to train for and win a gold medal in the Special Olympics. There is a solidarity that we share with others when we realize that we are not alone in our suffering. When we hear the stories of those who have gone through difficult times, we are reminded that we are not the first to encounter such suffering. Suffering is something common to all of us, and when we meet a "fellow sufferer," a bond is forged. This is especially true when we come to understand that the Son of God and the Mother of God both endured much suffering.

When you pray the rosary, you enter into all of the major milestones in Jesus's life. From the beginning, you first experience the joyful mysteries, followed by the luminous mysteries that touch on Jesus public ministry. You move through the sorrowful mysteries of suffering and on to the glorious mysteries that include the resurrection. Yet although the rosary encompasses so much, there is a beauty in its simplicity. St. John Paul II said in an Angelus message, "The Rosary is my favorite prayer. A marvelous prayer! Marvelous in its simplicity and its depth. In the prayer we repeat many times the words that the Virgin Mary heard from the Archangel, and from her kinswoman Elizabeth."[9]

When you pray the rosary you literally walk the passion of Christ with his mother. We are all familiar with the suffering of Christ and the price he paid for our salvation, but what about his mother? One of the titles of the Blessed Virgin Mary is Our Lady of Sorrows, and every September 15, the Catholic Church recognizes her sorrow and suffering by focusing on what she endured for the salvation of the world.

A fruitful devotion is the Seven Sorrows of Mary. These Seven Sorrows, not to be confused with the sorrowful mysteries of the rosary, are:

> The Prophecy of Simeon (Luke 2:34–35) or
> the Circumcision of Christ.
> The Flight into Egypt, (Matthew 2:13).
> The loss of the child Jesus in the Temple (Luke 2:43–45).
> Mary meets Jesus on the way to Calvary.
> Jesus dies on the cross (John 19:25).
> The piercing of the side of Jesus, and Mary's receiving
> the body of Jesus in her arms (Matthew 27:57–59).
> The body of Jesus is placed in the tomb (John
> 19:40–42).[10]

By praying the rosary we are reminded that Christ is no stranger, and his mother, the Blessed Virgin Mary, cares for us as our Mother. By praying the Seven Sorrows of Mary we are reminded that Mary was not spared of suffering and we can take comfort knowing that we can turn to her with our sufferings and, as a perfect loving mother, she will comfort us.

With your own suffering and a rosary in hand, you have a template to conform your life to Christ, and you have a guide, the Virgin Mary, who has walked this familiar path before.

While the rosary yields a vast array of blessings, it can also act as a plumb line to conform your life to the Lord, especially in difficult times. St. John Paul II once said the "rosary beats the rhythm of human life."[11] I like that quote. If the rosary beats the rhythm of human life, then you can find yourself in the rosary on any given day of the week.

When you're suffering you will find a particular drawing of the heart to the sorrowful mysteries. That's the place where you can really spend extra time joining your will with Christ. Don't avoid the rosary when you're suffering; instead cling to it and go deep into its mysteries. One of the beautiful truths about the rosary is that the one who was at the foot of Jesus's cross was his mother. Jesus was accompanied by the Blessed Virgin Mary, who was told earlier that "a sword will pierce through your own soul also" (Luke 2:35). She knew she was going to suffer, yet she never left her Son's side.

Don't go through trials alone. Jesus gave his Mother to the Church while he was still on the cross for a reason (see John 19:26–27).

Are there suffering and trials in your home? Don't let Mary be a stranger! Take her into your home as your spiritual Mother and let her be with you and care for you in your suffering. Think about the cross you're carrying today. Who is at the foot of your cross? In the rosary, your loving mother, Mary, will be with you.

In recent years the Church has enjoyed a favorite devotion of Pope Francis called Mary Undoer of Knots. I like this devotion because sometimes I feel like my life is tied up in knots. A painting by Johann Georg Melchior Schmidtner, created around 1700, inspired this devotion. Pope Francis was inspired by the painting while a student in Germany and went on to promote a devotion to it in Latin America. The painting depicts the Virgin Mary undoing knots while standing on the knotted serpent.

Think about all the frustrating times in childhood when you had knots in your shoelaces. Your little fingers just couldn't get the job done, and soon you were crying out for your mother's help. Times have changed— most of us can tie our shoes very well now—but the needs in our lives are still there. Mary has a way of undoing the knots in your life. Somehow, some way, her hands are skilled in undoing knots that our feeble hands just can't seem to handle.

Johann Georg Melchior Schmidtner got the idea of Mary untying knots from a work by St. Irenaeus of Lyons entitled *Adversus haereses* (Against Heresies). In book 3, chapter 22, he describes a parallel between Eve and Mary, describing how "the knot of Eve's disobedience was loosed by the obedience of Mary. For what the virgin Eve had bound fast through unbelief, this did the virgin Mary set free through faith."[12]

Remember, one advantage you have when you walk with the Blessed Mother in the rosary is that she will undo the knots of your life and help you conform your life to her Son. Another great advantage of the Blessed Mother being your prayer partner in suffering is that she also knows the final mysteries—and they are glorious!

Let's not forget one of the greatest advantages to praying the rosary in difficult times—its portability. It's like having your spiritual mom with you at all times. Sitting in the doctor's office, driving in traffic, waiting to pick up the kids at soccer, you can pray. You can pray the rosary anywhere, and the minute you start off with "I believe," you've built a sanctuary in time. You can be in the middle of the busiest schedule or craziest circumstances, and the rosary you hold in your hands can create a sanctuary where you can isolate yourself with Christ and his Mother.

Make a practice of praying the rosary in the trials of life, and let your children or grandchildren or friends join you in clinging to Jesus and the Mother of Sorrows, Mary.

8. Let the Saints Come Marching into Your Less-Than-Ideal Day!

Grieving over a lost loved one can produce fear-like symptoms. It can make you feel out of sync and almost disoriented. So often when we suffer, we vacillate between wanting to be left alone in our pain and hoping to be with people who care. When human companionship seems overwhelming, we can turn to the saints. The saints are those brothers and sisters who have run the race and now know something about the topic of suffering and grace. Like a good neighbor they will not impose themselves on you, but they certainly will join you if invited. Their wisdom is invaluable because it comes from lives of struggle and hearts that came to know Christ in the midst of the struggles.

The Church teaches that "by canonizing some of the faithful, i.e., by solemnly proclaiming that they practiced heroic virtue and lived in fidelity to God's grace, the Church recognizes the power of the Spirit of holiness within her and sustains the hope of believers by proposing the saints to them as models and intercessors. "The saints have always been the source and origin of renewal in the most difficult moments in the Church's history." Indeed, "holiness is the hidden source and infallible measure of her apostolic activity and missionary zeal" (CCC 828).

The constant witness of the saints confirms the truth of Romans 8:28: "We know that in everything God works for good for those who love him." Imagine what this would mean if you truly believed this. Just like the saints, you can be confident that God is working during your less-than-ideal days. This perspective on life gives you a multidimensional view of reality. You have an insider's scoop on how things will turn out.

St. Thomas More, shortly before his martyrdom, consoled his daughter: "Nothing can come but that that God wills. And I make me very sure that whatsoever that be, seem it never so bad in sight, it shall indeed be the best."[13] And Dame Julian of Norwich said: "Here I was taught by the grace of God that I should steadfastly keep me in the faith...and that at the same time I should take my stand on and earnestly believe in what our Lord shewed in this time—that 'all manner [of] thing shall be well.'"[14]

One great advantage that we enjoy in our relationship with the saints is that when we study their lives, we are looking at their life's playbook and getting an inside look at how they succeeded. Experience is valuable, and the saints offer their life strategies to us in fraternal love. It is very affirming to look into the lives of those who have gone before us and study how they lived and how they dealt with difficult times. Very often we gain insight from the saints that is not only encouraging, but gives us practical ideas on what to do in the midst of our own suffering.

Living in communion with the saints and entering into a familial relationship with them is similar to a young boy who aspires to play football that gets invited to hang out with Peyton Manning of the Broncos or Aaron Rogers of the Green Bay Packers. To have access to winners who are our brothers or sisters is priceless!

If we are willing to expand our scope in terms of relationships with the saints, we will also enjoy a constant reminder that we're not alone in our suffering. St. Paul tells us that the Church is like a body and every part is vitally important. We are so joined together in Christ that "if one member suffers, all suffer together; if one member is honored, all rejoice together" (1 Corinthians 12:26). Think about that! Your suffering is known by and even affects the saints. When one member of the body suffers, it's like dropping a rock in a pond—the ripples travel to and fro and are felt on all shores. Because we're all affected by even one person's suffering, we can all be a part of helping and encouraging others by praying for them and offering comfort in their time of need.

One of the common denominators of the saints is that, while many of them suffered, in the end they were victorious. They just seemed to know how to get the victory in the midst of the pain. Many of them have written diaries and books on what they went through and how their sufferings were salvific. Many saints knew what it meant to surrender themselves to suffering, both physical and moral. St. Thérèse of Lisieux wrote about her suffering and how she embraced it in her autobiography, *The Story of a Soul.* Blessed Mother Teresa wrote about the moral suffering she endured, unbeknownst to the rest of the world, in *Come Be My Light.*

And of course St. John Paul II offers a goldmine on suffering in his Apostolic Letter, *Salvifici Doloris.* If *Salvifici Doloris* is not a part of your library, race out and buy it. My copy is well-worn and thoroughly annotated, and it enjoys a prominent place on my library shelf.

To have access to men such as St. Maximilian Kolbe who gave up his life for another man in a Nazi concentration camp is to rub shoulders with a hero. To read the writings of and ask for the prayers from men like St. Augustine and St. Thomas is an immense treasure. Heaven is filled with holy women who have a tender heart towards the suffering on earth. St. Kateri Tekakwitha knows what it was like to live out the faith in an atmosphere hostile to the gospel. St. Katharine Drexel took an interest in the Native American and African American community and became well acquainted with their suffering. For those who have suffered as a result of infidelity, St. Mary Magdalene stands in your corner, pulling for you to walk in holiness and experience the healing power of Christ's forgiveness.

Over the years the Catholic Church has recognized certain saints who are supporters of particular areas of employment or struggles. For example, St. Maximilian Kolbe is the patron saint of addicts. St. Francis de Sales is the patron saint of authors. St. Lucy is especially sought after by those who are blind. For those who suffer with headaches, St. Teresa of Avila is a close friend. Physicians often call on Saints Cosmos and Damian or St. Luke. If you search the Internet, you will find saints for almost every place and every life situation. Take five minutes and think about what you are going through right now. Search and I'll bet you will find a saint to call on. If you can't find what you're looking for, just say, "Tony, Tony, look around, something's lost and can't be found," and St. Anthony is sure to come to your rescue. Go ahead—make a new friend today!

9. Keep an Eternal Perspective.
We all have a God-given ability to imagine the future, but we need to use that power to go even further and contemplate

eternity. Knowing that eternity with Christ, complete with pain-free living, is a future reality is a great comfort when you are dealing with pain. It's a little like being weighed down with tasks on Wednesday and then contemplating the weekend when you'll be able to rest and relax.

The writer of Ecclesiastes wrote, "[God] has put eternity into man's mind" (Ecclesiastes 3:11). Being created in the image and likeness of God, humankind is capable of some pretty impressive things. God is the same yesterday, today, and forever. If you look at yesterday, God was there and is there. He is present today, and he exists in all our tomorrows. God exists outside of time; he is constant and does not change. To a much smaller degree, we are capable as created beings to live in our yesterdays, our present, and our tomorrows. This is unique to human beings, and while it can be helpful at times, it can also paralyze us—particularly as it pertains to suffering. For many, the thought of experiencing pain and suffering combined with the knowledge that we are eternal beings can cause great distress in the mind and soul. What if I end up suffering with this malady for the rest of my life? What if the next forty years are spent in pain?

There are two things that you can do to combat the temptation to enter a state of despair when contemplating time. First of all, it is important to realize that suffering is temporal. For the Christian, suffering will end when they will enter into the beatific vision—that is, being with God forever. There will be an end to the battles we face, but until then we can do something with our suffering.

The second thing you can do is practice what I call "spiritual judo." Judo is a martial art that uses the momentum of an opponent to defeat him. If your opponent is throwing a punch toward your face, you can use his momentum to take him down by grabbing his arm and throwing him to the floor to pin him. What looked like your enemy (i.e., his fist coming at you at thirty miles an hour) will be used for your victory. The force of the attack on you becomes a counterforce to take down your opponent.

In the same way, because we have eternity in our hearts, in the midst of pain we can sometimes be a bit fearful about how long this suffering will last. Here's where spiritual judo comes into play. Take that fear of time and use it for your victory. Do what Jesus said: "Do not lay up for yourselves treasures on earth, where moth and rust consume and where thieves break in and steal, but lay up for yourselves treasures in heaven, where neither moth nor rust consumes and where thieves do not break in and steal" (Matthew 6:19).

In other words, take the temporal force of suffering's punch and turn it into an eternal reward. How? By grabbing it, embracing it, and—by an act of your will—joining your suffering to the suffering of Christ on the cross. Pin your suffering down to the mat by offering it up in union with Christ for a treasure in heaven.

10. Be Merciful and Show Forgiveness
When Christians correctly understand suffering, they will consciously begin looking for opportunities to relieve suffering by extending mercy to those around them. Mercy is a virtue that influences our priorities in such a way that we become instruments of God, extending his compassion to others with the hopes of alleviating suffering and misfortune. Simply put, mercy is love when it encounters suffering.

Typically the Catholic Church has divided the works of mercy into two kinds: corporeal (that is, bodily) and spiritual. There are many ways that we can extend mercy and love to those who have come upon difficult times. You can make a difference in the lives of those who are having a less-than-ideal day. The *Catechism* teaches: "[Human] misery elicited the compassion of Christ the Savior.... Hence, those who are oppressed by poverty are the object of *a preferential love* on the part of the Church" (CCC 2448).

You can get involved in your city's homeless shelters, or you can sponsor a child overseas. Our family has visited a wonderful local ministry that sends meals to the hungry overseas. This is something the whole family can get involved with together. You can also become educated on public policy and government initiatives. Your government spends your money on many projects that come under the banner of corporeal works of mercy. Take some initiative and play a role in where that money will be spent.

Every week in our parish we hear at the announcements at the end of mass, announcing the funeral schedule. The announcements are not made simply to keep us aware of what is happening in the parish, they are to give all of us an opportunity to do a work of mercy. Many people in our parish extend charity and kindness to those families who have lost loved ones. Attending a funeral or preparing food for a funeral as well as the days after a funeral are wonderful acts of mercy.

God also gives us many opportunities to extend mercy to our family and friends who are struggling with emotional and spiritual needs. Many times the needs that people face are not so evident from the outside, but they remain very painful on the inside. Being willing to talk with and pray for others is a welcome salve on sensitive wounds.

Throughout the course of life there will be times when you are hurt physically, but there will also be times when you are crushed by something someone said or something that happened to you that left you devastated. We all know that life seems unfair at times, and we have even been warned that we could be hurt by relationships. However, when betrayal, deception, or lies come our way, often we feel blindsided. It is at the point of pain that you will have a choice as to what you're going to do with that interaction that left you devastated.

How many of us can identify with this story? Things are fine with you and your brother-in-law, but then one Thanksgiving during the family get-together, he says something to you that kind of stings. You thought that what was said was wrong and unjust, but you let it pass. Days turn into weeks and weeks turn into months, and now your relationship has changed. What started off as you feeling offended has now turned into a full-blown grudge. You want payment; you want him to make it right. What God wants, however, is forgiveness.

The most difficult part of being a Christian is not teaching sacramental prep to young people, or cooking at the Fall Festival, or being on the finance committee. The hardest part of being a Christian is picking up your cross and dying to yourself as you forgive someone who has wronged you. Forgiveness is key to dealing with moral suffering; it offers the believer the opportunity to do something constructive with the pain.

When we bury our pain in our heart, it has a way of mani-festing in our life that is very destructive, not only to us personally, but to our loved ones as well. The human heart is not made to live with unforgivingness.

The Lord has given us the opportunity to share in his suffering for the greater good, but he has also shared another unique attribute of his: the ability to forgive. At the heart of forgiveness is the concept of releasing others for the pain they have inflicted upon you. Sticks and stones do break bones and yes, words do hurt. Rather than carrying an offense in your heart, which will only fester and cause more problems, take that offense to the cross and offer it up. Release the person who has hurt you. By doing so, you are saying, "Jesus paid the price for this particular sin, and I choose to join my pain to his cross that paid the price. In addition, I no longer expect the one who hurt me to pay; I release them and choose to love them."

CONCLUSION

You picked up this book because you wanted to find meaning in your suffering. Yes, in your suffering there is an immeasurable treasure. But the treasure will stay in your chest if you don't do something with it. Your task now is to live every day to the fullest. From the low-grade frustrations and annoyances to the life-threatening crises, you must exercise your will and consciously offer up your suffering and join it to the cross of Christ. By saying "I'm all in" when it comes to suffering, you are exercising your will and changing lives. This simple yet at times difficult step of faith can make a big difference in your life. In the words of my good friend Fr. Mike Schmitz: "Suffering without Christ just hurts. But suffering with Christ can transform the world."[1]

While we remain open to the miraculous healing power of Jesus, we remain open to the transformative power of suffering, too. We Christians can be compared to a man playing cards who carries in his hand two jacks. Nothing can take two jacks of the same color. If we are healed, we win by playing one jack; if we suffer, we win by playing the other. With this new understanding of suffering, you can trump whatever life throws at you. Just like St. Paul, you can say, "I can do all things in him who strengthens me" (Philippians 4:13).

Begin now to see your suffering as a gift infused with meaning, heavenly cash that can be spent on others. With your newfound understanding of the value of redemptive suffering, you can live your life in a new way. With the sure knowing that pain and suffering is a unique opportunity to love as Christ loves, you can begin to live 100 percent of your life. No longer will you live 40 percent of life and simply put up with 60 percent. Everyday can be an ideal day—a gift to God—when you know that your life counts for something greater than yourself and you have the hope of eternity with Christ deep in your heart. Now, go offer it up!

Notes

Foreword

1. C.S. Lewis, *The Problem of Pain* (San Francisco: HarperOne, 2001), p. 91.

Chapter One

1. Kathleen Craig, "Second Life Land Deal Goes Sour," *Wired,* May 18, 2006.
2. Eddie Makuch, "Professor Argues That WoW Can Be a 'Religious Experience,'" Gamespot, August 20, 2014.
3. Charles J. Chaput, *Render Unto Caesar: Serving the Nation by Living Our Catholic Beliefs in Political Life* (New York: Image, 2009), p. 75.
4. Peter Kreeft, *Making Sense Out of Suffering* (Cincinnati: Servant, 1986), p. 64.
5. Kreeft, p. 64.
6. Kreeft, p.65.
7. Kreeft, p.65.
8. St. John Paul II, *Salvifici Doloris,* I, 3.
9. *The Diary of Saint Maria Faustina Kowalska: Divine Mercy in My Soul* (Stockbridge, Mass.: Marian, 2010), p. 54.
10. *Salvifici Doloris,* II, 7.
11. *Salvifici Doloris,* II, 8.
12. *Salvifici Doloris,* II, 8.

13. *Salvifici Doloris,* II, 8.
14. *Salvifici Doloris,* II, 8.

CHAPTER TWO

1. "Ginormous," *Dictionary.com,* http://dictionary.reference. com/browse/ginormous.
2. "Pope John Paul II," *Wikipedia,* http://en.wikipedia.org/wiki/ Pope_John_Paul_II.
3. Vatican Insider, "The death of Deskur, Wojtyla's 'Pope Maker,'" September 11, 2011, Pope John Paul II Forum, http:// jp2forum.org/john-paul-ii-news/187/09-11-11/.
4. Charles Krauthammer, "Rick Ankiel, The Return of the Natural," *The Washington Post,* August 17, 2007.
5. Charles Krauthammer, Fox News Reporting Special (COMPLETE) 'A Life That Matters' – 10-25-13, https://www. youtube.com/watch?v=w4fQN1Czu_Q.
6. Fulton Sheen, *Life Is Worth Living* (San Francisco: Ignatius, 1999), p. 134.

CHAPTER THREE

1. Adapted from Scott Hahn, *A Father Who Keeps His Promises: God's Covenant Love in Scripture* (Cincinnati: Servant, 1998), pp. 70–71.
2. See *Confessions of St. Augustine,* book 2, chapters 1–10.
3. Fulton Sheen, *Way to Inner Peace* (Boston: St. Paul's, 1994), p. 59.
4. See Hahn, *A Father Who Keeps His Promises.*
5. *Salvifici Doloris,* II, 6.
6. C.S. Lewis, *The Problem of Pain* (San Francisco: Harper Collins, 2002).

CHAPTER FOUR

1. *Salvifici Doloris,* III, 12.
2. *Salvifici Doloris,* II, 10.
3. *Salvifici Doloris,* II, 10.

4. *Salvifici Doloris*, II, 12.

5. *Salvifici Doloris*, II, 12.

CHAPTER FIVE

1. *Salvifici Doloris*, III, 13.

2. *Salvifici Doloris*, IV, 13.

3. *Salvifici Doloris*, IV, 14.

4. *Dei Verbum*, Dogmatic Constitution on Divine Revelation, 10.

5. *Dei Verbum*, 11.

6. *Dei Verbum*, 13.

7. Stephen D. Benin, *The Footprints of God* (New York: State University of New York Press, 1993), p. 1.

8. Scott Hahn, *Scripture Matters* (Steubenville, Ohio: Emmaus Road, 2003), p. 2.

9. St. Thomas Aquinas, *Summa Theologica* I, 1, 10. Christians Classics Ethereal Library, http://www.ccel.org/ccel/aquinas/summa.FP_Q1_A10.html.

10. "Gianna Beretta Molla," *Wikipedia*, http://en.wikipedia.org/wiki/Gianna_Beretta_Molla.

11. *Salvifici Doloris*, V, 19.

CHAPTER SIX

1. Augustine, quoted in Angelo DiBerardino, *We Believe in One Holy Catholic and Apostolic Church* (Downers Grove, Ill.: InterVarsity, 2010).

2. "*Chariots of Fire*," *Wikipedia*, http://en.wikipedia.org/wiki/Chariots_of_Fire.

3. *Salvifici Doloris*, V, 20.

CHAPTER SEVEN

1. *Story of a Soul: The Autobiography of St. Thérèse of Lisieux*, 3rd ed., trans. John Clarke, O.C.D. (Washington, D.C.: ICS, 1996), p. 79.

2. John Paul II, *Salvifici Doloris*, V, 27.

3. Marguerite Duportal, *How to Make Sense of Suffering* (Manchester, N.H.: Sophia Institute, 2005), p. 80.

4. Duportal, p. 82.
5. Fulton J. Sheen, *Calvary and the Mass* (New York: Alba, 2010), p. 62.
6. Quoted in Mark J. Zia, *The Enduring Faith and Timeless Truth of Fulton Sheen* (Cincinnati: Servant, 2015).
7. Fulton Sheen, *Peace of Soul*, (Liguori, Mo.: Liguori, 1996), p. 219.
8. Sheen, *Peace of Soul*, pp. 227–228.
9. Arthur McGill, *Suffering: A Test of Theological Method* (Philadelphia: Westminster John Knox, 1982), p. 63.
10. Laura Sobiech, "Fly a Little Higher: How God Answered One Mom's Small Prayer in a Big Way," Kindle edition.
11. Brother Lawrence, *The Practice of the Presence of God*, Fourth Conversation (Radford, Va.: Wilder, 2008), p. 23.
12. *Salvifici Doloris,* V, 26.

CHAPTER EIGHT
1. See Peter Kreeft, *Making Sense Out of Suffering* (Cincinnati: Servant, 1986), pp. 96–97.
2. Laura Sobiech, *Fly a Little Higher: How God Answered a Mom's Small Prayer in a Big Way* (Nashville: Thomas Nelson, 2014), Kindle edition.
3. Sobiech, from the Author's Note.
4. Sobiech.
5. Sobiech.
6. See John Eldredge, *Wild at Heart* (Nashville: Thomas Nelson, 2001), pp. 10–14.
7. *Salvifici Doloris,* IV, 14.
8. Dietrich Bonhoeffer, *Prisoner of God: Letters and Papers from Prison* (New York: Macmillan, 1961), p. 105.
9. *Salvifici Doloris,* VI, 27.
10. *Salvifici Doloris,* VI, 26–27.

CHAPTER NINE
1. *The Diary of Saint Maria Faustina Kowalska: Divine Mercy in My Soul* (Stockbridge, Mass.: Marian, 2010), p. 24, n. 47.

2. John Paul II, *Reconciliation and Penance*, 10.
3. *Reconciliation and Penance*, 18.
4. *Reconciliation and Penance*, 15.
5. *Reconciliation and Penance*, 16.
6. From the new Roman Missal.
7. *The Rediscover: Hour*, Relevant Radio, 3/20/15, http://www. relevantradio.com/rediscover-hour.
8. John R. Henderson, "Demographics of the Titanic Passengers: Deaths, Survivals, Nationality, and Lifeboat Occupancy," http://www.icyousee.org/titanic.html.
9. St. John Paul II, *Angelus*, October 29, 1978.
10. "Our Lady of Sorrows," *Wikipedia*, http://en.wikipedia.org/ wiki/Our_Lady_of_Sorrows.
11. St. John Paul II, *Angelus*.
12. "Mary Untier of Knots," *Wikipedia*, http://en.wikipedia.org/ wiki/Mary_Untier_of_Knots#cite_note-2.
13. *The Correspondence of Sir Thomas More*, ed. Elizabeth F. Rogers (Princeton, N.J.: Princeton University Press, 1947), letter 206, lines 661–663 (quoted in CCC 313).
14. Julian of Norwich, *The Revelations of Divine Love*, trans. James Walshe, S.J. (London, 1961) pp. 99–100 (quoted in CCC 313).

CONCLUSION

1. Fr. Mike Schmitz, phone conversation with author.

ABOUT THE AUTHOR

Jeff Cavins is director of evangelization for the Archdiocese of
Saint Paul and Minneapolis, the creator of the popular Great
Adventure Bible Study series and the founding host of EWTN's
weekly program *Life on the Rock*. He is an international
speaker and the author of several books, including *Walking
with God: A Journey through the Bible*.